Fancy Sips & Party Dips

Fancy Sips & Party Dips

recipes by

Nancy L. Lockhart

NODIN PRESS

Design, layout Todd Marx
Illustration Brian Santos
Photography Gage S. Lockhart

ISBN: 978-1-935666-27-1

Nodin Press, LLC
530 N Third St.
Suite 120
Minneapolis, MN 55401

Table of Contents

Introduction

Meatball Appetizers

Dips

Spreads

Canapés

Cheese Balls

Assorted Appetizers

Sandwiches

Cheesecakes

Alcoholic Punches

Non-Alcoholic Punches

Hot Cocktails, Alcoholic & Non-Alcoholic

Introduction:

Planning a Cocktail Party?

This book contains helpful tips and information to guarantee that your evening will be a success.

First the Basics

What is the occasion? Is it purely for pleasure? How many guests will you invite? How many guests can you afford to invite?

Consider which guests will guarantee that your gathering will be interesting and memorable.

Once you have decided how many guests to invite and have chosen them carefully, it's time to focus on the menu, drinks, and decorations. Allow the food and drinks to take center stage. Dress up your room with the most elegant flower arrangements you can afford. Light the room with candles, and play some nice music (soft jazz?) in the background.

Planning your menu will naturally be determined by your budget. Even on a limited budget, it is possible to provide an elegant, yet simple selection of party food for your guests. Orchestrate an appetizer party with ease by preparing a buffet. A fairly standard formula is twelve appetizers per person. If you're inviting ten people you'll need a total of about 120 appetizers. If you're making six different appetizers you'll need twenty of each to keep your guests happy.

If the guest list has fewer than forty-five people, plan on providing six different appetizers. When the appetizers are the entire meal, offering some substantial entrees such as meatballs, cold sliced roast beef, and ham are a must. For smaller gatherings of eight to ten guests, three different appetizers are suitable. For fourteen to sixteen guests, plan on serving four to five different appetizers.

Savory Tea Sandwiches are not just for afternoon teas. They also go well at cocktail parties.

Tips on Making Tea Sandwiches

- Choose thinly sliced good quality sandwich bread with a light grain. Pepperidge Farm very thin sliced bread in white or wheat is what I prefer for making tea sandwiches.

- Spread each piece of bread with soft butter or cream cheese to seal it from moist fillings.

- Remove the crust before cutting the sandwiches to size.

- Once they've been assembled, cut the sandwiches into quarters or triangles. Some people enjoy cutting tea sandwiches into decorative shapes with a cookie cutter, but I seldom do because too much of the sandwich goes to waste.

- If you're making the sandwiches in advance, arrange them, uncut, on a tray lined with damp paper towels. Cover them with more damp paper towels and wrap them in plastic. Then chill. When you're ready to serve them, remove the crusts, quarter the sandwiches, and garnish. You'll find they're easier to cut when chilled.

Veggies, crackers, and chips served with tasty dips are inexpensive and fill people up. Cheese balls go further than cubed cheese.

Marinated vegetables are an attractive alternative to the platters of raw vegetable with Ranch dressing that are so often served.

Bowls of nuts and snack mixes are simple to set out and invariably popular.

Tiny, open face canapés are easy to make and appealing.

Meatballs and cocktail sausages can be served from a chafing dish or crock pot, simmering in a complimentary sauce.

The Perfect Cheese Platter

When it comes to a party, cheese platters are among the most popular choices for an appetizer. Cheese platters should always include a variety of soft and hard cheeses, both sharp and sweet. A well-chosen and balanced cheese platter can be a very intense and memorable experience. You don't need to be a cheese expert to assemble one. Just do a little research and develop a plan before you began your shopping.

What cheeses should you purchase and how much?

The number of cheeses you'll need will depend on the number of guests you're serving, how elaborate you want your platter to be, and how much you want to spend. Presenting three different cheeses on a platter is pretty standard. When cheese is the centerpiece of your party, five or more cheeses might be required. Plan on two to three ounces of cheese per guest.

Cheese Platter Themes

Having a theme makes the process of selecting cheeses easier and will also "tie" your platter together. For example, you could provide a sampling of cheeses that are all made with one type of milk, such as cow, goat, or sheep. You might decide to offer cheeses from a specific country such as Spain or Italy. Or you might decide to select cheeses from different countries that have similar flavors, such as Gorgonzola (Italy), Roquefort (France), and Stilton (England). It can also be fun to serve three or four similar cheeses, such as soft-ripened Brie and Camembert.

Arranging Your Cheese Platter

When arranging your cheeses, keep in the mind that the mildest cheese ought to be sampled first. "Soft" cheeses such as the rich and creamy Brie or buttery Camembert should precede "semi-soft" cheeses such as Gouda, Havarti, Muenster, Jack cheeses and Mozzarella. Flavors get more intense with "hard" cheeses like Cheddar, Gruyere, Pecorino Romano, and Parmesan. Finally, the most intense cheeses will be the "bleu" cheeses such as Bleu d' Auvergne, Stilton, Gorgonzola, and Roquefort.

Never crowd your cheese platter. Serve slices of a baguette or crackers in a separate basket. Offer a different knife for each cheese. Be sure to serve the cheese at room temperature. Cheese can actually sit at room temperature, lightly covered, for a couple of hours before serving. It's a good idea to serve a broad range of nuts and fruits such as grapes, berries, slices of apple or pears on hand as well, and perhaps some assorted cold cuts.

Pairing Cheese with Beer

Most people immediately think of pairing wine with cheese, but what about beer and cheese? Not only does this combination have an ancient heritage, but beer pairs better with some cheese flavors than wine does. The nutty butter and caramel aromas found in many aged cheeses are also present in malty beers like brown ales, stouts, and porters. Lighter beers like pilsner and wheat beers often compliment mild cheeses well. The reverse, however, is not true. Pairing an intense beer with a strong cheese is often just too much flavor to handle. It's better to pair a more mellow beer with a big complex cheese.

Here are some more specific guidelines:

Young, fresh cheeses: Chevre, Burrata and fresh Mozzarella pair well with lighter beers.

Sharp cheeses: Sharp cheddars, Double Gloucester, Grafton Village Cheddar, and Tillamook Cheddar pair well with lightly hopped, bitter beers.

Aged, nutty cheeses: Asiago, Emmentaler, Gruyere, Parmigiano-Reggiano require malty beers.

Assorted bleu cheeses: Danish Blue, Stilton, Gorgonzola, Roquefort pair well with sweet wines, and require sweet beers, Belgian ales and stouts.

Pairing Cheese with Wine

Throwing together wine and cheese pairings doesn't have to be complicated, so long as the pairing enhances the flavor of the cheese as well as the wine. As a rule, you should serve a cheese you like to eat with a wine you like to drink. First, figure out what type of wine will be served, whether it is a full bodied red, a dessert wine, or a crisp white.

Medium-bodied red wines include Pinot Noir and some Zinfandels and Merlots. Choose a cheese that has a good amount of butterfat and has been aged for a little bit to accompany these wines. Choices would include Gruyere, aged goat cheeses such as Boucheron, soft cheeses such as Camembert, young and sharp cheddars, young and creamy Swiss cheese, and Muenster.

Full bodied red wines include Cabernet Sauvignons, many Merlots and Zinfandels, estate-bottled red wines of Bordeaux, and Chianti. Aged cheeses go well with these wines. Good choices would include Asiago, Brie and Camembert (very ripe), aged cheddar and English Farmstead cheeses, Chevre, Pecorino Romano, Parmigiano-Reggiano, Provolone, sheep's milk cheeses (aged, salty, nutty), and aged Gouda.

Although red wines go with cheese more easily, there are several cheeses that can be served wth white wine.

White Wines including Chardonnay, Pinot Blanc, Riesling, Gewürztraminer, Pinot Gris, Sauvignon Blanc, and Semillon.

Cheeses to pair with these wines include creamy cheeses, like Brie, and creamy-to-hard white cheese such as Swiss (best served with Gewürztraminer and Riesling). Mild Cheddar go well with Pinot Gris), mozzarella is best with Sauvignon Blanc and Semillon, and goat's-milk cheeses with Sauvignon Blanc and Semillon.

Über-rich triple cheese crèmes like Pierre Robert, Brillat-Savarin and St André should be served with sparkling wine or champagne. Mold-donned and bleu-veined cheeses pair up best with ports and dessert wines.

A Few Final Tips for Planning Your Cocktail Party

- It's better to make too many appetizers than not enough, especially if the buffet food is the meal.
- You don't have to stock a full bar for a cocktail party.

Champagne and/or wine, beer, water and sodas are equally impressive and acceptable.

- Another option is to serve wine, beer, etc., with a specific selection of three to six different cocktails, stocking only the spirits and mixers needed to make those cocktail recipes. Most guests are thrilled with that.

- Allow twice as many glasses as you have guests. Make sure you have plenty of ice. Have a good selection of non-alcoholic drinks, with coffee (decaf and regular) being offered toward the end of evening.

Party Punch Tips

When considering punch for your party, figure ten people to the gallon. The amount of punch or number of cocktails a guest drinks will vary, of course. Allow for the length of the party and the strength of the punch. Figure that your guests will consume at least two 4-ounce servings per hour for the first two hours, and one drink per person per hour after that.

How to make a festive party ring for your punches

Place some sliced fruit, such as lemons, oranges, and limes, in the bottom of a large round mold. Add some maraschino cherries or colorful frozen fruit as preferred. Slowly pour ginger ale, lemonade, a fruity dessert wine, or even plain charged water, until it just covers the fruit. Freeze. Remove the mold from the freezer and add more of the same fruit and some mint leaves. Slowly fill with the original liquid of your choice and freeze again.

Float this frozen ring in the punch bowl with your preferred party punch recipe. Make a few of these in advance, so you'll have extra when replenishing your punch bowl. Remember, when designing your frozen party ring, to choose a fruit/liquid combination that will compliment the flavor of the punch.

There you have it. These helpful tips make planning a cocktail party so simple. With the recipes selected for this book, you will be able to transform an average social gathering into something really special.

Appetizers

Crock Pot Swedish Meatballs

1 pound ground beef
1 pound ground pork or veal
1 cup fresh bread crumbs
½ cup buttermilk
½ cup finely chopped onion
1 teaspoon dill weed
¼ teaspoon allspice
¼ teaspoon nutmeg
1 teaspoon salt
2 eggs (beaten)
⅓ cup all purpose flour
¼ teaspoon white pepper
3 cups beef broth
1 cup heavy cream

Combine bread crumb with buttermilk. Allow to soak for 10 minutes. Mix with the meats, onion, dill weed, allspice, nutmeg, salt and eggs. Shape into 1 inch balls. Arrange in a single layer on a large baking pan, brown in a 400 degree oven for 15 minutes. Remove from oven and put into crock pot. Combine flour, white pepper, beef broth and heavy cream in medium sauce pan, heat over medium heat, using a wire whisk to mix. Simmer until gravy thickens. Pour gravy over meatballs. Cover and cook on low for a couple of hours. Place on buffet table.

Makes 30 Meatballs

Meatballs with Mint Dipping Sauce

2 pounds ground beef
2 eggs, beaten
1½ cups finely chopped onion
1½ cups bread crumbs
2 tablespoons chopped fresh mint
2 teaspoons minced garlic
2 teaspoons salt
3 tablespoons lemon juice
Oil for frying

Mint Dipping Sauce

1 cup plain yogurt
2 to 4 tablespoons fresh mint (finely chopped)
¼ cup finely chopped green onions
½ teaspoon granulated garlic
2 teaspoons minced fresh ginger

First prepare the Mint Dipping Sauce and refrigerate it.
Combine the yogurt, mint, green onions, garlic and ginger;
cover and chill until ready to use. Mix all the meatball
ingredients together by hand until well combined. Form
the mixture into 1½ inch balls. Pour just enough oil into a
non-stick frying pan to cover the bottom and heat. Add the
meatballs and cook through, browning them on all sides.
Drain them on paper towels. Serve hot with chilled Mint
Dipping Sauce.

Makes 40 Meatballs

Spicy El Paso Meatballs

2 pounds ground beef
1 teaspoon dried hot chili peppers
2 tablespoon Cajun seasoning
1 tablespoon Worcestershire Sauce
1 tablespoon chopped cilantro
¼ cup finely chopped onion
½ cup fresh bread crumbs
½ cup buttermilk
2 eggs
1 cup Hickory barbeque sauce
1 cup peach preserves

Combine bread crumbs with the buttermilk, and allow too soak for 10 minutes. Thoroughly mix with the ground beef, chili peppers, Cajun seasoning, Worcestershire sauce, cilantro, onion and eggs. Shape into 1 inch meatballs. Arrange on a large baking sheet and bake in a preheated 375 degree oven for 25-30 minutes.

While meatballs are baking, combine the barbeque sauce and peach preserves in a sauce pan. Cook over medium heat. When meatballs are done, remove from oven and drain off fat. Place in a serving dish and pour the sauce over them. Insert fancy toothpicks and serve.

Makes 20 Meatballs

Mincemeat & Deviled Ham Meatballs

1½ pound ground beef
2½ ounce can deviled ham
1 teaspoon crushed dried chilies
½ cup panko bread crumbs
½ teaspoon salt
2 beaten eggs

Mincemeat Mixture:

1 22-ounce can mincemeat
½ cup apple cider
1 tablespoon balsamic vinegar

Combine all meatballs ingredients in a large bowl. Shape into 1 inch meatballs. Arrange in a single layer on a large baking sheet. Bake in preheated 350 degree oven for about 20 minutes.

While meatballs are baking, combine mincemeat mixture in sauce pan and heat through.

Place meatballs into a 2½-quart crock pot and pour mincemeat mixture over them. Put on low setting for 1-2 hours. Add to buffet table.

Makes 20 Meatballs

Savory Meatballs

2 pounds ground beef
1 small onion, grated
½ cup oatmeal
2 eggs
¼ teaspoon ginger
¼ teaspoon nutmeg
¼ teaspoon allspice
1 teaspoon balsamic vinegar
2 cups steak sauce
⅔ cups brown sugar
Salt & pepper to taste

Combine with the ground beef, the onion, egg, oatmeal, spices, teaspoon of sugar, and ½ cup of the steak sauce. Add the salt and pepper. Form into 1½ inch balls and bake at 400 degrees in a shallow pan for about 20 minutes. Pour off the fat. In a sauce pan, combine 1½ cups of the steak sauce, ⅔ cup of the brown sugar, and mix well. Cook over medium heat until sugar dissolves. Add the meat to coat well. Serve on platter with toothpicks in each ball.

Makes 20 Meatballs

Asian Influenced Appetizer Meatballs

3 pounds ground beef
2 eggs
½ cup bread crumbs
¾ cup soy sauce
¼ cup brown sugar
2 cloves garlic, minced
1 teaspoon ground ginger

In a large bowl, combine all of the ingredients and shape into 1-inch meatballs. Arrange in a single layer in a large baking pan. Put into 350 degree oven and bake uncovered for about 30 minutes, turning once. Transfer balls to chafing dish.

Makes 24 Meatballs

Sausage-Cheddar Meatballs

2 cups all purpose baking mix of your choice
1 pound bulk hot Italian sausage
4 cups (16 ounces) sharp cheddar cheese (shredded)
½ cup Parmesan Reggiano cheese (shredded)
½ cup milk
¼ cup fresh Italian parsley (chopped)

Preheat oven to 350 degrees. Mix together all ingredients. Shape mixture into one inch balls. Place on a large baking sheet. Bake 20 to 25 minutes, or until golden brown. Remove from pan and serve warm with a nice barbecue or chili sauce for dipping.

Makes 40 Meatballs

Turkey Meatballs

4 cups finely chopped cooked turkey meat
1 medium onion grated
1 cup bread crumbs
1 cup of buttermilk
2 eggs well beaten
1 tablespoon Dijon Mustard
1 teaspoon salt
¼ teaspoon white pepper
¼ teaspoon nutmeg
1 clove garlic minced
Butter of margarine for browning meatballs

Combine the turkey, onion, bread crumbs, milk, eggs, garlic and spices. Shape into small balls about the size of walnuts. Brown turkey balls in the butter. Then transfer them to a well-greased chafing dish. Serve with toothpicks.

This is a great way to transform left-over turkey into elegant appetizers.

Makes 36 Turkey Meatballs

Oriental Meatballs

2 pounds ground pork
2-5 ounce cans water chestnuts, drained and chopped
1 bunch green onions, chopped including tops
1 cup bread crumbs
2 eggs slightly beaten
2 tablespoons soy sauce
½ teaspoon ginger
¼ cup corn starch

Mix together all ingredients. Form into 1" balls and bake at 400 degrees in a preheated oven for about 15 to 20 minutes turning occasionally. Remove from oven, drain on paper towels.

Sauce:

½ rice vinegar
⅓ cup & 1 teaspoon sugar
1 tablespoon soy sauce
1 can low sodium beef broth
½ teaspoon ginger

Simmer all ingredients together in a small to medium size sauce pan. Combine ¼ cup cornstarch and ¼ cup water. Add this to mixture and thicken like gravy. Place meatballs into a chafing dish and pour sauce over them. Stir this all together so that the balls are well glazed. Serve with toothpicks.

Makes 20 Meatballs

Cranberry Meatballs

4 pounds ground beef
4 eggs
2 teaspoons salt
¼ teaspoon pepper
Pinch of allspice
½ cup onion (finely chopped)
2 cups dry bread crumbs
½ cup water
32 ounces jellied cranberry sauce
4 tablespoons brown sugar
2 tablespoons lemon juice
1½ cups chili sauce

Combine ground beef, eggs, salt, pepper, onion, bread crumbs and water. Shape into meatballs and brown in a medium skillet; drain. Combine cranberry sauce, brown sugar, lemon juice and chili sauce in sauce pan. Simmer; stirring until smooth. Place meatballs in a five-quart crock pot and pour sauce over them. Cover cook on low for 3 to 4 hours.

Makes 40 Meatballs

Ham & Sauerkraut Balls

1 cup ground ham
1 cup grated Swiss or cheddar cheese
¼ cup diced green onions
¼ cup diced green pepper
2 cups sauerkraut (drained & squeezed as dry as possible)
1 egg
1 tablespoon prepared spicy brown mustard
¼ cup grated Parmesan cheese
Breading set-up (flour, egg, beaten with a little milk, panko bread crumbs)
Oil for deep fat frying

Mix all meatball ingredients well. Firmly shape into 1 inch balls and put through breading procedure (dredge in flour, dip in egg mixture, and roll in bread crumbs). Cook in deep fryer at 350 to 375 degrees for 3 to 5 minutes or until golden brown. Remove from fryer and drain on paper towels. Place on a serving dish, insert fancy toothpicks.

Makes 20 Meatballs

Ham & Ground Beef Meatballs

1 pound ground beef
1 pound ground ham
2 eggs
1 cup bread crumbs
1 cup buttermilk
½ cup vinegar
1 cup brown sugar
1 tablespoon prepared mustard
½ cup water

Combine the meat, eggs, milk and bread crumbs. Shape into 1½ inch balls. Combine vinegar, brown sugar, mustard and water. Pour over balls in a large pan. Bake at 350 degrees for about one hour. Serve in chafing dish with toothpicks.

Makes 25 Meatballs

Easy Cocktail Meatballs

2 pounds ground beef
½ cup bread crumbs
1 package dry onion soup mix

Sauce:

½ cup apple jelly
½ teaspoon oregano
1 14-ounce bottle ketchup

Mix ground beef, bread crumbs, and soup mix together and form into 1-inch balls. Bake in a 400 degree preheated oven for about 15 to 20 minutes until browned.

While meatballs are baking, mix sauce ingredients together in a medium sauce pan and heat through.

Remove meatballs from oven and drain off fat. Place balls into a chafing dish and pour on the special sauce. Heat through, stirring once or twice, and serve with toothpicks.

Makes 25 Meatballs

Hot Italian Meatballs

2 pounds hot Italian sausage
1 medium onion grated
1 teaspoon minced garlic
1 cup bread crumbs
1 large egg
½ cup grated Parmesan cheese
1 teaspoon salt
1 teaspoon pepper

Sauce:

1 16-ounce can tomato paste
1 cup water
½ cup red wine
2 beef bouillon cubes
2 teaspoons Italian seasoning, crushed
1 tablespoon brown sugar
¼ teaspoon crushed red pepper

Mix meatball ingredients together. Shape into 1 inch balls. Bake in shallow pan in preheated 400 degree oven for about 20 minutes. Simmer sauce ingredients for 30 minutes. Pour sauce into a crock pot. Add baked meatballs. Cook on low for 1 hour. Place on buffet table.

Makes 20 Meatballs

Cranberry Meatballs à la Sharon

1½ pounds ground beef
1 cup bread crumbs
1 small onion, grated
Salt & pepper to taste

Sauce:

1 6½-ounce bottle chili sauce
1 16-ounce can jellied cranberry sauce
1 tablespoon grated orange peel
¼ cup brown sugar
Dash of cayenne pepper

Mix together ground beef ingredients. Shape into 1½ inch balls. Bake on shallow pan in 400 degree preheated oven for about 15-20 minutes. Remove balls from oven and allow to drain on paper towels. Combine sauce ingredients in a sauce pan and simmer until all lumps are dissolved. Add drained meatballs to this mixture and simmer. Place in crock pot and simmer. Place on buffet table.

Makes 20 Meatballs

Exotic Coffee Balls

1½ pounds ground beef
1 egg beaten
1 teaspoon Worcestershire Sauce
¼ cup grated onion
1 tablespoon instant coffee
¼ teaspoon mace
1 teaspoon salt
¼ teaspoon pepper

Combine all of the above ingredients and shape into 1 inch balls. Put into shallow baking pan and bake at 350 degrees for about 20 minutes. Spear with toothpicks and serve hot.

Makes 20 Meatballs

Sour Cream Taco Dip

2 cups sour cream
1 package taco seasoning mix (hot or mild)
1 tablespoon of chopped green chilies
1 tablespoon grated onion

Mix all ingredients together and chill. Serve with tortilla chips.

Olive Dip

8 ounce package cream cheese, softened
¼ cup finely chopped ripe olives
1 tablespoon green onion chopped fine
1 teaspoon "Beau-Monde" seasoning

Combine ingredients; mix well. Chill for a few hours. Serve cold with crackers.

Shrimp Dip

8 ounce package cream cheese, softened
4½-ounce can of shrimp
¼ cup of chill sauce
½ teaspoon horseradish
⅛ teaspoon cayenne pepper

Drain shrimp and chop finely. Combine well all remaining ingredients. Mix thoroughly. Chill.

Pink Clam Dip

1 8-ounce can minced clams
2 8-ounce packages cream cheese, softened
1 tablespoon chopped pimento
¼ teaspoon garlic power
⅛ teaspoon cayenne pepper
¼ teaspoon onion power
1 tablespoon clam juice
1 tablespoon chili sauce

Allow cream cheese to soften at room temperature. Drain the clams, saving the juice. Beat with electric mixer the cheeses, spices, pimento, clam juice and chili sauce. Mix in clam meat. Serve with raw vegetables or crackers.

Pizza Dip

1 8-ounce package cream cheese, softened
1 small can pizza sauce with meat or sausage
½ teaspoon crushed Italian seasoning
1 tablespoon grated Parmesan cheese

Blend pizza sauce and cream cheese together. Add remaining ingredients and blend well. Serve immediately with your favorite chips or crackers.

Chutney Dip

1 8-ounce package cream cheese, softened
1 tablespoon heavy whipping cream
¼ teaspoon curry power
½ cup fine minced chutney

Drain the chutney very thoroughly. Blend well with other ingredients. Chill and then serve. Warning-Add no more chutney than what has been designated or the dip will be too sweet, and therefore, ruined

Pimento Cream Cheese Dip

1 8-ounce package cream cheese, softened
2 tablespoons chopped pimento
1 tablespoon grated onion
½ teaspoon horseradish
¼ teaspoon minced garlic
1 tablespoon chili sauce
1 teaspoon of Worcestershire Sauce
1 teaspoon milk

Beat all ingredients together well. Cover and chill for a few hours, or can be served at room temperature. Serve with raw vegetables or crackers.

Curry Dip

1 8-ounce package cream cheese, softened
1 tablespoon curry power
2 tablespoons applesauce
1 teaspoon lemon juice
Dash cayenne pepper

Beat all above ingredients with electric mixer, until smooth. Chill. Serve with crackers or vegetables.

Everybody's Favorite Onion Dip

1 8-ounce package cream cheese, softened
1 small to medium onion, grated
2 teaspoons "Salad Supreme" seasoning
Dash of cayenne pepper
1 teaspoon Worcestershire Sauce
1 tablespoon sour cream

Beat all ingredients together with an electric mixer until smooth. Pour into serving dish. Serve with chips.

Blue Cheese Dip

1-8 ounce package cream cheese, softened
4 ounces blue cheese
1 tablespoon grated onion
1 tablespoon sour cream
Dash of cayenne pepper

Beat all ingredients together with an electric mixer. Chill and then serve with chips or crackers.

Wine Blue Cheese Dip

2 4-ounce packages blue cheese
4 ounces cream cheese, softened
1 teaspoon Worcestershire Sauce
¼ cup dry white wine
1 teaspoon minced garlic

Crumble blue cheese into blender. Add remaining ingredients and blend at low speed. Turn to high speed and blend until completely smooth. Serve with crackers.

Sour Cream Vegetable Dip

2 cups sour cream
¼ cup mayonnaise
¼ cup cucumber, seeded and grated
1 teaspoon dill weed
¼ teaspoon Beau Monde seasoning
Dash of white pepper

Mix all ingredients together. Chill well and serve with raw vegetables. It's best to make this dip the night before.

Cottage Cheese Dip

12 ounce carton cottage cheese (small curd)
½ cup of salad dressing (Miracle Whip)
1 small onion (grated)
2 teaspoons dill weed
2 teaspoons Worcestershire Sauce
¼ teaspoon seasoning salt
¼ teaspoon garlic power
⅛ teaspoon cayenne pepper

Blend in food processor. Chill several hours. Serve with celery sticks.

Italian Parmesan Cheese Dip

1 8-ounce package cream cheese, softened
1½ tablespoons grated Parmesan cheese
½ teaspoon of Italian seasoning
¼ cup milk (start with 1 tablespoon and add more if needed)
¼ teaspoon garlic powder
Salt & pepper to taste

Blend all ingredients together well. Pour into serving dish and serve with your favorite crackers.

Eggplant Dip (Poor Man's Caviar)

1 medium eggplant
1 tablespoon onion, grated
⅓ cup minced celery
½ cup ripe olives, chopped fine
4 tablespoons olive oil
2 tablespoons red wine vinegar
1 tablespoons sugar
¼ teaspoon salt
¼ teaspoon pepper

Preheat oven to 350 degrees. Bake eggplant for about one hour. When cool enough to handle, peel and chop coarsely. Put the eggplant in a bowl and add remaining ingredients, pulse for about two minutes in a food processor. Pour into serving dish and chill, or can be served at room temperature. Serve with pita crackers.

Horseradish Ham Dip

1 8-ounce package cream cheese, softened
3 tablespoons Cheez-Whiz
¾ cup cooked ham, finely chopped
1 tablespoon milk
1 tablespoon horseradish
Salt & pepper to taste

Combine cream cheese, Cheez Whiz, ham, milk and horseradish. Mix until well blended. Add a little more milk if mixture seems too thick. Serve with crackers. (very zippy)

Bacon Sweet & Sour Dip

1 8-ounce package cream cheese, softened
5 slices bacon, diced
Dash hickory smoke
1 teaspoon prepared mustard
¼ cup of sweet & sour sauce
chives

Cook bacon until crisp. Drain on paper towels. Combine cream cheese, mustard, sauce and Hickory Smoke until smooth. Mix in bacon. Chill for several hours, garnish with chives. Serve with crackers.

Bacon & Tomato Dip

1 8-ounce package cream cheese, softened
1 16-ounce can stewed tomatoes, drained & chopped
½ pound bacon, cooked crisp
1 tablespoon prepared mustard
⅛ teaspoon cayenne pepper
Dash of liquid smoke
3 tablespoons chopped green onion

Combine cream cheese, tomatoes, mustard, pepper and liquid smoke in a food processor. Pulse until blended. Remove from processor. Add bacon and green onion. Refrigerate for several hours. Serve with chips or crackers.

Spinach Dip

1 10-ounce package frozen chopped spinach,
        squeezed dry
1 cup of sour cream
1 cup of mayonnaise
1 8-ounce can water chestnuts, drained & chopped
fine
1 package Knorr's Vegetable Dry Soup Mix
2 bunches chopped green onions

Mix all ingredients and refrigerate 6 to 8 hours, covered. Pour into a round, hollowed-out loaf of bread. Cut-up the bread you removed from center of the loaf into bite-sized pieces, and use for dipping.

Guacamole Dip

2 large ripe avocados
1 cup sour cream
1 tablespoon grated onion
1 teaspoon of lemon or lime juice
1 clove of garlic crushed
1 teaspoon chili powder
1 teaspoon ground cumin
⅓ cup green chilies
¼ teaspoon salt
1 medium tomato chopped

Peel avocados and remove pits. Scoop out insides into a food processor. Add remaining ingredients, and pulse 2-3 times. You want a chunky texture. Pour into a bowl and chill. Replace pit into dip to prevent from turning brown. Serve with tortilla chips.

Hot Chili Bean Dip

1 16-ounce can pork & beans
1 16-ounce can stewed tomatoes, drained
1 medium onion, grated
2 teaspoons chili power (hot)
2 teaspoons ground cumin
2 teaspoons ground oregano
4 cloves minced garlic
⅛ teaspoon cayenne pepper
1 4-ounce can chopped green chilies
2½ cups of sharp cheddar cheese, grated
1 pound ground beef
Salt & pepper to taste

Brown ground beef, drain and put to the side. Into a food processor, combine beans, tomatoes, onion, spices and chili peppers. Blend for about 30 seconds. Mixture should be lumpy. Pour mixture into heavy saucepan. Add the cheese and ground beef. Heat through until mixture is hot and cheese is melted. Pour into chafing dish, serve hot with tortilla chips.

Seven-Layer Hummus Dip

1½ cups prepared hummus
¼ teaspoon ground cumin
1 clove garlic, minced
½ cup marinated sun-dried tomatoes, chopped
¼ cup chopped cucumber
Freshly ground black pepper to taste
2 tablespoons minced parsley
2 teaspoons minced parsley
2 teaspoons minced oregano
½ cup crumbled feta cheese
¼ cup chopped kalamata olives
¼ cup chopped green onion

Stir cumin and garlic into your prepared hummus. If your hummus is already strongly flavored, this step may not be necessary. Spread the prepared hummus in the bottom of a pie plate and top it with the chopped sun-dried tomatoes. Top those with cucumber and season cucumber with freshly ground black pepper. Sprinkle the feta over. Add the parsley and oregano. Sprinkle on the crumbled Feta cheese, olives and green onion. Cover and chill until ready to serve. Serve with crisp pita crackers.

Avocado-Olive Dip

3 avocados, peeled, seeded and mashed
1 can black olives, drained and thinly sliced or mashed
1 4-ounce can chopped green chilies or jalapeños
7 green onions, chopped
3 large tomatoes, peeled, seeded, and chopped
3 cloves garlic, minced
6 tablespoons extra-virgin olive oil
2 tablespoons lemon juice
5 basil leaves finely chopped

Into a food processor combine all the ingredients.
Refrigerate for 2 hours. Excellent served with corn chips.

White Bean Dip

2 15-ounce cans cannellini beans, drained & rinsed
4 cloves garlic
3 tablespoons fresh lemon juice
¼ cup olive oil
¼ cup fresh Italian Parsley leaves
2 teaspoons kosher salt
Freshly ground pepper to taste
2 teaspoons dried rosemary

Place the beans, garlic, lemon juice, olive oil, salt, pepper, and rosemary in a food processor. Combine until smooth. Add the parsley, and pulse until combined. Transfer dip to a serving bowl and drizzle with a little olive oil. Serve with pita chips.

Charlyn's Jalapeño Cheese Dip

1 pound Velveeta cheese, grated
1 16-ounce jar chunky salsa
1 pound round loaf sourdough bread
1 medium onion, grated
1 green pepper, chopped fine
1 4-ounce can chopped green chilies
1 4-ounce can diced jalapeño peppers
1 envelope taco seasoning mix

In heavy saucepan, sauté salsa, taco seasoning, onion, green pepper, green chilies, and jalapeño peppers. Add the grated cheese, simmer until melted. Cut off the top of bread and remove the center to create a bowl. Fill bread bowl with dip. Bake in preheated oven at 350 degrees for 30 minutes. Remove from oven. Serve with thinly sliced baguette.

Cheeseburger Dip

1 pound ground beef
1 small onion, finely chopped
1 16-ounce can refried beans
1 4-ounce can chopped green chilies
1 cup chili sauce
2 cups shredded Monterey Jack cheese
8 ounces carton sour cream

Sauté the ground beef and onion in a skillet, drain off the fat, and place the beef mixture in a crock pot. Stir in the refried beans, chilies, chili sauce and shredded cheese. Cover and cook on low for 2 hours. Just before serving, stir in the sour cream. Serve warm with tortilla chips.

Nancy's Mushroom Dip

1 8-ounce package fresh mushrooms, chopped
1 8-ounce package cream cheese
½ cup sour cream
1 medium onion, grated
1 clove minced garlic
2 tablespoons Worcestershire Sauce
¼ teaspoon thyme
½ teaspoon white pepper
2 tablespoons butter or margarine
Salt to taste

Place mushrooms into medium saucepan along with butter. Cook over low-to-medium heat, and continue cooking until mushrooms are very tender, and some of the liquid has cooked down. Add the rest of the ingredients, heat over low heat until hot. Remove from heat and pour into a serving dish. Serve immediately with raw vegetables or crackers.

Hot Bean Dip

1 8-ounce package cream cheese, softened
1 cup sour cream
2 16-ounce cans refried beans
½ 1-ounce package Taco seasoning
5 drops hot pepper sauce
2 tablespoons chopped parsley
¼ cup green onions, chopped
1 8-ounce package cheddar cheese, shredded

Preheat oven to 350 degrees. In a medium bowl, blend the cream cheese and sour cream. Mix in the refried beans, taco seasoning, hot pepper sauce, parsley, green onions, cheddar cheese and Monterey Jack cheese. Bake in the oven 20 to 30 minutes, until cheese is slightly browned. Serve with tortilla chips.

Deviled Ham Dip

1 4½-ounce can deviled ham spread
1 8-ounce package cream cheese, softened
1 tablespoon grated onion
1 teaspoon prepared spicy brown mustard
1 egg yolk (optional)
2 teaspoons Worcestershire Sauce

Blend ingredients in food processor until smooth and creamy. Chill and serve. (This tastes best when made the night before.)

Crock Pot Spinach &
Artichoke Cheese Dip

½ pound Swiss cheese, grated
½ pound Mozzarella cheese, grated
½ pound Parmesan Reggiano
1 8-ounce package cream cheese
1 cup mayonnaise
2 teaspoons Worcestershire Sauce
¼ teaspoon granulated garlic or garlic powder
1 10-ounce package frozen leaf spinach (thawed &
squeezed dry)
1 16-ounce can artichoke hearts (drained & chopped)

Combine all ingredients in a 2-quart crock pot. Cook on low
setting for 2 to 3 hours. Serve with pieces of crusty French
bread.

Layered Taco Spread

1 8-ounce package cream cheese, softened
1 cup sour cream
¼ cup "Miracle Whip" salad dressing
1 package taco seasoning
2 bunches chopped green onions with tops
½ head of lettuce, shredded
3 tomatoes, roughly chopped
1 tablespoon diced green olives
1 tablespoon diced black olives
1 cup grated cheddar cheese

Cream together cream cheese, sour cream, salad dressing and taco seasoning mix. Spread this mixture on a 9- or 12-inch square or round glass pan with sides. Cover with a layer of onions, then lettuce, then tomatoes, then olives, and finally, top with the grated cheese. Drizzle with hot taco sauce. Serve with taco chips.

Chicken Liver Cheese Spread

¾ pound chicken livers
¼ teaspoon minced garlic
1-8 ounce package cream cheese, softened
2 tablespoons sherry
¼ teaspoon thyme
2 tablespoons margarine or butter (for sautéing)
Salt & pepper to taste

Sauté chicken livers in butter, remove livers. Add sherry to the pan and scrape up the drippings. Into a food processor, put livers, drippings, cream cheese, thyme and garlic. Blend until smooth, season to taste with salt and pepper. Refrigerate. Serve with crackers or chips.

Wine Cheese Spread

1 3-ounce package cream cheese, softened
2 8-ounce packages soft sharp cheddar cold pack
        cheese food
1 tablespoon pimento, chopped fine
1 tablespoon grated onion
1 teaspoon horseradish
1 teaspoon Worcestershire Sauce
1 ounce sherry

Blend all ingredients in food processor until smooth. Serve at room temperature with crackers.

Smoked Oyster Cheese Spread

1 8-ounce package cream cheese, softened
2 4-ounce jars smoked oysters, chopped
2 tablespoons mayonnaise
2 tablespoons sherry
2 tablespoons minced green onion
2 teaspoons onion juice
½ teaspoon paprika

Mix above ingredients well. Pile into serving dish. Serve with crisp crackers.

Curried Cheese Spread

2 cups sharp cheddar cheese, grated
2 tablespoons chopped pimento
½ cup chopped green onion
1 teaspoon horseradish
2 teaspoons curry power
2 cloves garlic minced
½ cup mayonnaise

Combine all ingredients in a food processor. Blend well. Put cheese spread in a serving dish. Serve at room temperature with crackers.

Salmon Spread

1 16-ounce can of salmon (remove bones & drain)
1 medium onion, grated
1 teaspoon ground black pepper
1 tablespoon minced celery
1 tablespoon "Beau-Monde" seasoning
½ cup of mayonnaise
1 teaspoon Dijon style mustard
Chopped fresh chives (dried may also be used)

Combine all ingredients in a food processor except for chives. Blend until smooth. Spoon mixture into a bowl and garnish with chives. Chill for a few hours. Serve with crackers.

Tuna Spread

1 6½-ounce can of tuna, drained well
1 cup sour cream
1 tablespoon chopped green onion tops
1 teaspoon "Salad Supreme" seasoning
1 teaspoon sugar (optional)
¼ teaspoon black pepper
½ teaspoon "Beau-Monde" seasoning

Combine all ingredients, and mix well. Chill for a few hours and serve with crackers.

Beer Cheese Spread

1 pound extra-sharp cheddar cheese, finely grated
¼ cup grated onion
¼ teaspoon garlic power
1 tablespoon pimento, chopped fine
1 tablespoon chili sauce
1½ teaspoon Worcestershire sauce
¼ teaspoon cayenne pepper
1 teaspoon horseradish
6 ounces beer

Allow cheese to soften to room temperature. Combine ingredients in a food processor. Add the beer a little at a time until all the beer has been added and the mixture is light and fluffy. Pour into a heavy crock-type container. Cover and refrigerate at least one week to allow the flavors to ripen. Serve with crackers.

Bacon, Cheese & Chutney Torte

32 ounces high-quality extra-sharp shredded cheese
      at room temperature
2 cups chopped pecans
1 cup sweet minced onion
8 teaspoons Mayonnaise

Combine these ingredients and divide in half. Spread half of
the mixture evenly over the bottom of a 9 inch spring form
pan; set aside.

2 8-ounce packages cream cheese, softened
⅔ cups mango chutney
1 teaspoon cayenne pepper

Combine these ingredients in a bowl and mix thoroughly.
Spread over the cheddar cheese mixture and place in the
refrigerator to chill.

2 8-ounce packages cream cheese, softened
1 10-ounce package frozen chopped spinach, thawed
      and squeezed dry
6 slice of bacon cooked until crisp and crumbled
1 teaspoon granulated garlic
1 teaspoon salt

Combine these ingredients in a bowl and mix thoroughly.
Spread over chutney mixture. Top with the remaining half
of cheddar cheese mixture and cover with plastic wrap.
Refrigerate until ready to use. This freezes well, and can
be made several days in advance. Serve with assorted
crackers.

Layered Middle Eastern Spread

1 8-ounce package cream cheese
1 4-ounce package crumbled feta cheese
1 tablespoon Italian seasoning
1 cup shredded Parmesan cheese
1 (7.5 ounce) can Caponata (eggplant appetizer)
1 bunch green onion with tops, chopped finely
1 8-ounce jar marinated artichoke hearts, drained &
chopped

Combine cream cheese, feta, and Italian seasoning in a
food processor. Set aside. Line a 1-quart bowl with plastic
wrap, allowing 8 inches of wrap to extend up over the sides.
Layer ingredients in this order: half of the Parmesan, half
of the Caponata, half of the cream cheese mixture, the
green onions, olives, artichoke hearts, remaining Caponata,
remaining cream cheese, remaining Parmesan.

Fold plastic wrap over the top and refrigerate until firm and
ready to serve. The spread can be made as much as two
days in advance. To serve, remove from refrigerator and
unfold plastic wrap. Place serving platter face down on top
of bowl. Flip it over and remove the bowl. Carefully peel off
plastic wrap. Serve with pita chips or crackers.

Fantastic Easy Crab Mousse

1 2-pound package cooked crabmeat
1 8-ounce package cream cheese, softened
1 10¼-ounce can cream of mushroom soup
1 package unflavored gelatin
½ cup mayonnaise
½ cup sliced green onions
½ cup chopped celery

Lightly spray a 4-cup mold and set aside. Carefully clean the crabmeat of any shells or cartilage. In a medium saucepan over medium-low heat, combine cream cheese and mushroom soup; stir until well blended. Sprinkle gelatin over mixture; stir until well blended. Stir in mayonnaise until well blended. *Do not boil*. Remove from heat. Mix in sliced green onions and ½ cup chopped celery.

Pour crab mixture into prepared mold and refrigerate overnight. To un-mold, briefly dip mold in hot water, being careful not to let water run into the mold. Invert onto a serving platter and serve with assorted crackers. Can be made up too two days in advance.

Shrimp Mousse

1 can tomato soup
1 teaspoon lemon juice
1 teaspoon Worcestershire Sauce
1 8-ounce package cream cheese
1 envelope unflavored gelatin

Combine first four ingredients in a medium saucepan. Heat until hot, but *do not boil*. Take off heat and add envelope of unflavored gelatin. Then add:

½ cup chopped green pepper
½ cup chopped celery
½ cup chopped green onion
1 cup mayonnaise
1 lb finely chopped cooked shrimp

Pour into a greased two quart mold. Refrigerate overnight. Unmold and serve with crackers.

Salmon Mousse

1 pound freshly poached or canned Red Sockeye
  salmon
½ cup green pepper, diced
1 bunch of finely diced green onions with tops
3 tablespoons chopped fresh dill
1 tablespoon capers
½ cup mayonnaise
½ cup sour cream
1 8-ounce package cream cheese
¼ cup chili sauce
½ teaspoon dried crushed chili peppers
1 tablespoon lemon juice
½ cup white wine or Vermouth
1 envelope unflavored gelatin
1 greased or non-stick 6-cup mold

In a bowl combine salmon, green pepper, green onions, dill, capers, mayonnaise, sour cream and lemon juice. In a saucepan, melt the cream cheese and add the chili sauce and the dried crushed chili peppers. Cook over a low heat until mixture is smooth and creamy. Add this to the salmon mixture and pour everything into a food processor. Pour the wine into a small saucepan and add the gelatin. Stir with a wire whisk to disperse gelatin throughout the liquid.
Slowly heat the wine until gelatin dissolves. *Do not boil*.
Add the dissolved gelatin to the salmon mixture in the food processor. Blend well and pour into the greased mold. Refrigerate for six hours or overnight. Unmold onto a large serving dish. Garnish with fresh dill and sprigs of watercress. Serve with slices of baguette or cocktail slices of rye bread.

Clam Meat Canapés

1 7½-ounce can of minced clams, drained
2 tablespoon grated onion
1 teaspoon lemon juice
1 teaspoon Worcestershire Sauce
¼ cup mayonnaise
¼ teaspoon garlic power
¼ teaspoon thyme
salt & pepper to taste
10 slices of good quality white/wheat bread

Combine first eight ingredients. Spread on bread slices. Cut each slice into quarters and serve.

Makes 40 Canapés

Tuna & Cheese Canapés

1 6½-ounce can of tuna, drained
1 cup grated cheddar cheese
1 small onion, grated
1 tablespoon Dijon mustard
1 tablespoon lemon juice
¼ teaspoon thyme
salt & pepper to taste
1 dozen toast rounds

Combine in a bowl all ingredients except toast rounds. Spread on toast rounds and put in preheated broiler about 4 inches from heat. Broil until melted, about 5 minutes. Serve hot.

Makes 12 Canapés

Clam & Cheddar Cheese Canapés

1 8-ounce can minced clams, drained
¾ cup grated sharp cheddar cheese
1 tablespoon grated onion
1 tablespoon pimento, chopped fine
¼ cup mayonnaise
⅛ teaspoon cayenne pepper
salt to taste
12-15 toast rounds

Combine clams, cheese, onion, pimento, mayonnaise, pepper, and salt. Mix well. Spread on toast rounds and put in preheated broiler about 4 inches from heat. Boil until nice and melted, but not spilling onto broiler pan. Remove and serve hot.

Makes 15 Canapés

Tasty Velveeta Cheese Ball

1 8-ounce package cream cheese, softened
1 cup Velveeta cheese, shredded
1 cup sharp cheddar cheese, shredded
1 package dry onion soup mix
3 tablespoons sweet pickle relish, drained & squeezed dry
1 cup chopped pecans or walnuts for coatings

Blend the cheeses, soup mix, and pickles in a food processor. Cover and chill in a bowl overnight. The next day form into a ball and roll in the nuts. Allow to stand at room temperature for at least an hour before serving. Serve with your favorite crackers.

Swiss-Almond Cheese Ball

1 8-ounce package cream cheese
10 ounces Swiss cheese, shredded
2 teaspoons Worcestershire Sauce
½ teaspoon salt
½ teaspoon dry mustard
¼ teaspoon crushed dried red chili peppers
½ cup sliced almonds for garnish

In a food processor, combine cheeses, Worcestershire Sauce and spices. Process until well blended. Cover and chill in a bowl overnight. The next day, form into ball and roll in the almonds. Allow to stand at room temperature for at least an hour before serving. Serve with your favorite crackers.

Chili Cheddar Ball

1 8-ounce package sharp cheddar cold pack cheese
1 8-ounce package cream cheese, softened
1 teaspoon chill powder
1 teaspoon ground cumin
1 tablespoon chopped green chilies
1 teaspoon chopped pimento
¼ teaspoon garlic powder
¼ teaspoon cayenne pepper
8 ounces chopped nuts for garnish

Combine cold pack cheese food and softened cream cheese, mixing until well blended. Add remaining ingredients; mix well. Chill until firm. Form into ball and roll into chopped parsley, chopped nuts, or crushed tortilla chips. Serve as a spread with crackers.

Classic Cheese Ball

1 8-ounce package cream cheese, softened
1 cup sharp cheddar cheese, grated
4 ounces Roquefort cheese (room temperature)
1 small onion, grated
1 teaspoon granulated garlic
½ teaspoon dry mustard
2 long squirt of Worcestershire Sauce
¼ teaspoon Lawry's season salt
¼ teaspoon cayenne pepper
8 ounces chopped walnuts (for garnish)

Combine all ingredients well excluding nuts. Roll into ball.
Cover with chopped walnuts and chill. Before serving allow
to sit at room temperature for easy slicing. Serve with
crackers.

Pineapple Cheese Ball

2 8-ounce packages cream cheese, softened
1 8-ounce can crushed pineapple, drained
¼ cup chopped green onion
¼ teaspoon granulated garlic
½ teaspoon salt
½ teaspoon Worcestershire Sauce
⅛ teaspoon allspice
1 cup crushed pecans (for garnish)

Combine all ingredients excluding pecans. Chill overnight. Form into ball and coat the outside with the pecans. Serve chilled with crackers. Great taste sensation, something people will remember.

Bacon Cheese Ball

1 8-ounce package cream cheese, softened
1 cup shredded sharp cheddar cheese
6 bacon slices cooked crisp
1 tablespoon chopped green pepper
1 tablespoon grated onion
1 teaspoon horseradish
1 teaspoon Worcestershire Sauce
½ teaspoon dry mustard
A couple of drops of Hickory Smoke
Dash of cayenne pepper
Chopped fresh parsley (dried may be used) for coating
    ball

Blend together in food processor cream cheese, cheddar cheese, horseradish, mustard, Worcestershire Sauce and Hickory Smoke. Add onion, green pepper and bacon. Pulse three times. Chill overnight. Roll into chopped parsley. Allow to sit at room temperature before serving. Serve with crackers.

Salmon Ball

1 16-ounce can of salmon, drained well & flaked
1 8-ounce package cream cheese, softened
½ stick sweetened butter
1 tablespoon grated onion
1 tablespoon lemon juice
1 teaspoon horseradish
¼ teaspoon salt
Dash of thyme
Parsley & chopped nuts for garnish

Mix together all ingredients excluding the garnish. Cover and chill for a few hours or overnight. Shape into a ball and roll into the parsley and nuts. Serve with your favorite crackers.

Liverwurst & Cream Cheese Ball

1 8-ounce package good quality liverwurst
4 ounces cream cheese, softened
1 8-ounce package cream cheese, softened
¼ cup grated onion
2 teaspoons horseradish
¼ teaspoon mace
½ teaspoon garlic powder
¼ teaspoon salt
1 cup of finely chopped parsley

Combine the liverwurst, four ounces of cream cheese, onion, horseradish, mace and salt. Chill until firm. Form into ball. Spread eight ounces of softened cream cheese around the ball and roll into chopped parsley. Chill for a few hours. Serve cold with crackers. When presented, slice off the end piece to display the interior design.

Crab Cheese Ball

1 8-ounce package cream cheese, softened
1 8-ounce jar Cheez Whiz
1 teaspoon horseradish
2 teaspoons Worcestershire Sauce
2 teaspoons seafood seasoning (e.g. Old Bay)
1 bunch chopped green onions
2 tablespoons unsalted butter at room temperature
1 tablespoon fresh lemon juice
1 pound shredded crabmeat
1 cup chopped nuts

In a food processor, combine cream cheese, Cheez Whiz, horseradish, Worcestershire Sauce, seafood seasoning, butter and lemon juice. Process until mixed. Add to this the chopped green onion and crabmeat. Pulse a few times until blended. Do not over-mix. Roll in chopped nuts and refrigerate for several hours or overnight. Serve with your favorite crackers.

Gorgonzola & Craisin Cheese Ball

1 8-ounce package cream cheese, softened
1 cup (4 ounces) gorgonzola cheese
1 cup dried chopped craisins
1 teaspoon grated orange peel
¼ cup finely minced green onion
1 tablespoon finely chopped red bell pepper
¼ teaspoon cayenne pepper
¼ teaspoon kosher salt
1 cup finely chopped pecans

Into a food processor, combine the cheeses, grated orange peel, salt and pepper. Blend until smooth. Add the craisins, onion and bell pepper and pulse until mixed. Do not over-mix. Shape into a ball, wrap in plastic wrap and refrigerate overnight. Unwrap and roll into chopped pecans. Serve immediately with your favorite crackers or wrap and chill until ready to use.

Pecan & Date Cheese Ball

1 teaspoon ground mustard
1 teaspoon water
2 8-ounce packages cream cheese, softened
¼ cup mayonnaise
¼ teaspoon ground nutmeg
2 cups shredded cheddar cheese
1 cup chopped dates
1 cup chopped pecans

In a small bowl, dissolve the mustard in water; let stand for 10 minutes. In another bowl, beat cream cheese and mayonnaise until smooth. Add nutmeg and mustard mixture. Stir in cheese and dates, and chill. Roll in chopped pecans. Serve with crackers.

Dried Fruit & Cheddar Cheese Ball

2 8-ounce packages cream cheese, softened
¼ cup chopped pitted dates
¼ cup chopped apricots
¼ cup chopped prunes
¼ cup chopped craisins
1 cup finely chopped pecans or walnuts

Place everything except the nuts in a food processor. Pulse until combined. Do not over-process. Form into ball. Wrap in plastic wrap and chill in refrigerator until firm. Roll ball into chopped nuts. Serve immediately or keep in refrigerator until ready to use. Serve with crackers.

Sweet, Spicy & Savory White Vermont Cheddar Cheese Ball

½ cup dried apple slices

3 teaspoons Apple Jack brandy

1 tablespoon pure maple syrup

6 slices of bacon fried crisp & crumbled

1 8-ounce package cream cheese, softened

1 10-ounce package white cheddar cheese, shredded

¼ cup chopped green onion tops

¼ teaspoon dry mustard

¼ teaspoon cayenne pepper

1 tablespoon dark brown sugar

1 cup chopped pecans

In a small bowl, combine apple slices with the brandy and maple syrup. Finely chop in a food processor. Next, add the cream cheese, cheddar cheese, dry mustard and cayenne pepper. Process until well blended. Add the onions and pulse about four times. Combine brown sugar, bacon and pecans. Shape mixture into a cheese ball and roll into bacon-pecan mixture. Cover with plastic wrap and chill until firm. Serve with crackers and apple slices.

Date, Walnut & Blue Cheese Ball

1 8-ounce package cream cheese, softened
1 cup (4 ounce) blue cheese, crumbled
1 tablespoon sour cream
5 or 6 pitted medium dates, finely chopped
¼ cup minced shallots
1 teaspoon grated lemon peel
½ teaspoon salt
¼ teaspoon cayenne pepper
2 tablespoons chopped Italian parsley
1 cup finely chopped walnuts

Combine cream cheese, blue cheese, and sour cream in food processor. Blend until smooth and creamy. Add the dates, shallots, lemon peel, salt and pepper. Process until well combined. Form cheese mixture into a ball, wrap in plastic wrap and chill overnight. Unwrap cheese ball and roll it in the parsley-nut mixture until evenly coated. Serve immediately or cover and refrigerate until ready to use. Serve with your favorite crackers.

Pimiento Cheese Ball

2 cups Swiss cheese, shredded
2 cups cheddar cheese, shredded
1-8 ounce package cream cheese, softened
½ cup sour cream
½ cup chopped onions
1 2-ounce jar of pimientos
2 tablespoons sweet pickle relish
10 slices of bacon, cooked crisp, drained and crumbled
½ cup pecans, finely chopped
1 dash pepper
¼ cup parsley, finely chopped

Let Swiss and cheddar cheeses come to room temperature. In a large bowl beat together cream cheese and sour cream till fluffy. Beat in Swiss cheese, cheddar cheese, onion, pimiento, pickle relish, half of the bacon, ¼ cup of the pecans, salt and pepper. Cover and chill until firm. Shape into ball on wax paper. In a small bowl combine remaining bacon, pecans, and parsley. Place mixture on a clean sheet of waxed paper. Roll cheese ball in mixture to coat. Wrap and chill for at least six hours or overnight. Remove from refrigerator and let stand at room temperature for 30 minutes. Serve with crackers, artisan bread, or assorted vegetables and fruits.

Tuna Cheese Ball

2 6½-ounce cans solid white tuna, drained & flaked
2 8-ounce packages cream cheese, softened
6 tablespoons sweet pickle relish, drained & squeezed
¼ cup minced onion
1 teaspoon Worcestershire Sauce
½ teaspoon hot sauce
½ teaspoon salt
¼ teaspoon granulated garlic
1 cup fresh parsley, chopped

Combine together first eight ingredients to form a ball.
Roll into the chopped parsley. Refrigerate several hours or
overnight. Serve with your favorite crackers.

Spinach, Cheese Squares

1 pound whole milk ricotta cheese
2 large eggs
¼ cup chopped green onions with tops
2 ounces sharp cheddar cheese, shredded
3 tablespoons melted butter
1 tablespoon all purpose flour
½ teaspoon salt
½ teaspoon granulated garlic
¼ teaspoon freshly ground black pepper
⅛ teaspoon dry red pepper flakes
20 ounces frozen spinach, thawed & squeezed dry
1 ounce Parmesan cheese, shredded

Preheat oven to 350 degrees. Spray a 9 inch square baking pan with a non-stick cooking spray. In a bowl, mix together the ricotta cheese, eggs, and green onions until well combined. Mix in cheddar cheese, melted butter, flour, salt, garlic, black pepper, and red pepper flakes until thoroughly mixed. Fold in spinach. Pour mixture into prepared baking pan. Sprinkle with Parmesan cheese. Bake 45 to 55 minutes until top is golden. Remove from oven and allow to cool to room temperature. Cut into small squares.

Makes 24 Appetizers

Debbie's Snappy Buns

8 hamburger buns, split in half
6 ounces cheddar cheese, grated
6 ounces Monterrey Jack cheese, grated
1 small onion, grated
⅔ cups chili sauce
½ cup water chestnuts, chopped
½ pound of bacon, cooked crisp & crumbled

Combine the cheeses, onion, chili sauce, and water chestnuts. Add the bacon and mix all ingredients in bowl. Place the buns on a cookie sheet, spoon some cheese mixture over each bun. Put into a preheated broiler for about five minutes or until cheese melts. Watch closely; serve hot.

Dill Pickle, Cream Cheese, Corned Beef Pinwheels

2 8-ounce packages cream cheese, softened
8 large size kosher dill pickles
16 ounces sliced corned beef

Pat pickles dry with paper towels. Spread cream cheese over a slice of meat. Place a pickle on one end of meat slice and roll-up. Repeat this process until all the pickles have been rolled. Cover and chill for at least 2 hours or overnight. Cut into 1 inch slices and spear with a toothpick.

Makes 36 Pinwheels

Santa Fe Smoked Salmon & Cream Cheese Wraps

1 8-ounce package cream cheese, softened
1 pound smoked salmon, sliced very thin
1 small jar roasted red bell peppers, sliced
1 small jar capers
1 4¼-ounce can chopped ripe olives, drained
1 avocado, peeled, pitted, and sliced thin
½ cup chopped green onion tops
1 small jar julienned sun-dried tomatoes (packed in oil)
1 package 10-inch flour tortillas

Spread a thin layer of cream cheese evenly over each tortilla. Layer a small amount of the rest of the ingredients evenly over the surface of the cream cheese. Roll-up tightly. Wrap each roll in plastic wrap and refrigerate for several hours or overnight. Unwrap and slice each tortilla diagonally into 1 inch pieces. Skewer each wrap with a wooden toothpick and arrange on a platter.

Makes 48 Wraps

Roast Beef Pinwheels

4 large thin slices medium-rare roast beef
4 ounces cream cheese, softened
2 teaspoons prepared horseradish (or to taste)
¼ teaspoon granulated garlic
½ teaspoon salt

Combine cream cheese, horseradish, garlic and salt in a medium bowl. Mix well. Spread the mixture evenly over each slice of roast beef. Roll each slice tightly and wrap them individually in plastic wrap. Refrigerate for at least two hours. Unwrap the rolls and cut into ½ inch slices. Spear with toothpicks and arrange on a serving platter.

Makes 36 Pinwheels

Fresh Tomato Bruschetta

10 Italian Plum tomatoes, diced
¼ cup chopped sun-dried tomatoes (packed in oil)
3 cloves minced garlic
¾ cup fresh basil leaves, coarsely chopped
1 teaspoon fresh lime juice
⅓ cup extra-virgin olive oil
Salt & coarsely ground pepper to taste
1 pound loaf French bread, cut into 1-inch slices
Aged Balsamic vinegar (for garnish)

Preheat oven to 475 degrees. In a medium bowl, mix together tomatoes, sun-dried tomatoes, garlic, basil leaves, lime juice, olive oil, salt, and pepper; set aside. Brush one side of each slice of bread with extra virgin olive oil. Place the slices oil-side down on a cooking sheet and toast them in the oven until golden brown. Top each slice of bread with tomato mixture. Drizzle with balsamic vinegar and serve.

Makes 16 Appetizers

Bacon, Spinach & Cheese Swirls

1 package (17.3 ounces) puff pastry sheets, thawed
1 10-ounce package frozen chopped spinach, thawed
      & squeezed dry
½ cup Muenster cheese, shredded
½ cup grated Parmesan cheese
¼ cup finely chopped green onions
6 thick-cut slices bacon, diced & cooked crisp
¼ teaspoon granulated garlic
1 egg, beaten

Preheat oven to 400 degrees. Combine the Muenster cheese, Parmesan cheese, onion, bacon and garlic in a medium bowl. Roll one pastry sheet into a 13 x 11 inch rectangle and brush with beaten egg. Spread one half of the bacon-spinach-cheese mixture over the sheet. Roll up like a jelly roll, starting with the long side. Repeat procedure with remaining pastry sheet. Cut both rolls into ½-inch slices. Place slices on lightly greased baking sheets and brush them with beaten egg. Bake for 15-20 minutes, or until golden brown. Serve hot or wrap rolls in plastic wrap and refrigerate for up to two days.

Makes 40 Appetizers

Southwest Tortilla Wraps

2 8-ounce packages cream cheese, softened
1 cup sour cream
1 4¼-ounce can chopped green chilies, drained
1 4¼-ounce can chopped ripe olives, drained
1 cup (4 ounces) sharp cheddar cheese, shredded
2 tablespoons salsa (plus salsa for dipping)
½ cup chopped green onions
1 teaspoon granulated garlic
1 cup chopped fresh arugula
5 10-inch flour tortillas

In a large bowl combine first four ingredients. Beat until blended. Add the rest of the ingredients, except for the tortillas and mix until blended. Spread mixture evenly over the surface of each tortilla. Roll-up tightly. Wrap each roll in plastic wrap and refrigerate for several hours or overnight. Unwrap, and cut each tortilla into 1-inch diagonal slices. Skewer each wrap with a wooden toothpick. Serve with Salsa.

Makes 48 Wraps

Vidalia Stuffed Fried Bread

12 frozen dinner rolls, thawed
¼ pound sliced bacon, chopped
2 cups thinly sliced Vidalia onions
1¼ cups whole ricotta cheese
½ cup grated Parmesan cheese
½ cup grated fresh Mozzarella cheese
¼ cup chopped fresh chives
1 teaspoon onion powder
½ teaspoon salt
½ teaspoon pepper
⅛ teaspoon nutmeg
1 egg, beaten
Vegetable oil
Favorite Marinara sauce for dipping (if preferred)

In a large, heavy skillet, cook the bacon until crisp, but not too crisp. Remove from pan and set aside on paper towels to drain. Add the onions to the pan and cook until soft and brown, about 15-20 minutes. Remove from pan and set aside on paper towels to drain.

Combine the ricotta, Parmesan, mozzarella, chives, onion power, salt, pepper, and nutmeg together in a large bowl. Add the bacon and onion to the mixture. Mix together well. Taste and adjust seasonings if preferred.

Pour oil 2 to 3 inches deep into a large heavy skillet (I use cast-iron), heat oil to medium (350 degrees). Using a rolling pin, flatten each dinner roll into a 5-inch circle. Place a heaping tablespoon of filling onto one half of each circle. Brush edges of dough with beaten egg. Fold each circle in half, forming a turnover. Press with a fork to seal the edges.

Gently put the turnovers into the hot oil. Do not overcrowd. I don't fry more than two at a time. Use a large spoon to pour some of the hot oil over the turnovers as they cook, to help them to cook evenly and puff up. When they're puffed and golden, gently remove with a slotted spoon to drain on paper towels. Arrange the warm turnovers on a large platter and serve with your favorite marinara sauce for dipping.

Makes 12 Turnovers

Nachos

1 pound ground beef
1 package taco seasoning mix
1 16-ounce can refried beans
1 large bag of tortilla chips
1 cup hot pepper cheese, shredded
1 cup sharp cheddar cheese, shredded
1 16-ounce jar salsa
1 16-ounce carton sour cream
½ cup chopped green onions

Preheat oven to 425 degrees Layer tortilla chips on a cookie sheet. In a sauce pan, brown ground beef with the taco seasoning mix. Add the refried beans, mix together, and heat through. Combine the cheeses with the spices. Spread the refried beans over the tortilla chips and top with the cheese mixture. Garnish with the green onions and pop into the oven. Bake until the cheese has melted. Remove and serve immediately.

Hot Brie Quesadillas

4 8-inch flour tortillas
1 pound Brie cheese cut into thin slices
1 cup chopped ripe tomatoes
1 large avocado, peeled, seeded, and finely chopped
½ cup finely chopped fresh cilantro
½ cup green onions, finely chopped
Hot pepper sauce to taste
Sour cream for garnish
Finely chopped green onions for garnish

If your skillet is not non-stick, lightly spray with non-stick cooking spray. Heat your skillet (I like to use my cast-iron skillet) on low heat. Place one flour tortilla in the skillet and arrange ¼ of the Brie slices on top. Add ¼ of the tomatoes, avocado, cilantro, onions hot pepper sauce, salt, and pepper. Top with another tortilla and very carefully, using a wide spatula, flip the quesadilla over and cook another 2 to 4 minutes, or until the cheese is just melted. Remove from the skillet and cut each quesadilla into quarters. Top each quarter with a tablespoon of sour cream and sprinkle with chopped green onion. Serve hot.

Makes 16 Appetizers

Stuffed Jalapeño Poppers

16 jalapeño chili peppers
12 ounces cream cheese, softened
8 slices of bacon, cooked until crisp
3 tablespoons grated Parmesan cheese
1 teaspoon granulated garlic
2 cups (8 ounces) sharp cheddar cheese, shredded

Fry the bacon until crisp and set aside. Preheat oven to 350 degrees. Rinse and dry the peppers. Slice off the stem and cut in half lengthwise. Take a small knife and scrape out the seeds and membranes. Remember, the heat is in the seeds and membranes. In a medium bowl, add the cream cheese, parmesan cheese, garlic, and mix well.

Crumble the bacon and combine with the cream cheese mixture until well blended. Spray a cookie sheet with a non-stick spray. Using a spoon, mound the cream cheese mixture into each pepper half. Sprinkle with cheddar cheese and press into cream cheese so it sticks. Place the stuffed jalapeño peppers on the cookie sheet. Place cookie sheet in oven and bake for 25 to 30 minutes or until golden brown. Serve immediately.

Makes 32 Poppers

Cheddar Appetizer Nibbles

4 ounces sharp cheddar cheese
⅓ cup butter or margarine, melted
1 tablespoon grated onion
1 tablespoon milk
1 tablespoon prepared mustard
1 cup finely crushed potato chips
¾ cup flour
⅛ teaspoon cayenne pepper

Combine cheese, butter, milk, mustard, pepper and onion.
Mix well. Combine potato chips and flour. Add to creamed
mixture and mix well. Take rounded teaspoons full of dough
and shape into balls. Place on ungreased cookie sheets.
Flatten slightly with a fork. Bake in preheated oven at 375
degrees 12-14 minutes or until golden brown. Serve warm or
at room temperature.

Marinated Vegetables

½ head cauliflower
½ pound fresh large mushrooms
4 stalks broccoli
4 stalks celery
4 large carrots
3 green peppers
6 green onions
1 16-ounce bottle Italian dressing

Wash all vegetables and clean. Cut into pretty, bite-sized pieces. Marinate over night in 1 to 2 cups of Italian dressing. Add a little sugar and extra vinegar for a zesty tang. Serve in an attractive bowl or on a relish tray. Guests can help themselves, enjoying the marinade or dipping pieces in a vegetable dip. (See, for example, the recipe for Sour Cream Vegetable Dip on page 21.)

Jalapeño Pie

2 cans green chilies, chopped
8 jalapeños, seeded and chopped
1 pound Monterey Jack cheese, grated
1 pound cheddar cheese, grated
12 eggs, beaten
¼ teaspoon garlic powder

Butter a 9-inch baking pan. Spread chilies and peppers in bottom of dish. Spread cheese over peppers. Add garlic power to beaten eggs and pour over cheeses. Bake at 350 degrees in oven for 30 minutes. Cut into small squares and serve.
Makes 12 servings

Hot Cocktail Sausages

1 12-ounce can tomato puree
¼ cup cider vinegar
¼ cup firmly packed brown sugar
1 tablespoon prepared mustard
1 teaspoon chili power
¼ teaspoon allspice
⅛ teaspoon cayenne pepper
1 16-ounce package of cocktail wieners

Mix all of the above ingredients except for the wieners. Simmer uncovered in a heavy skillet, stirring frequently. Add the wieners and simmer uncovered for about 10 minutes. Pour into chafing dish and spear with toothpicks.

Stuffed Mushrooms

12 large mushrooms
3 tablespoons butter
1 small onion, grated
1 6½-ounce can chicken meat
1 cup fine soft bread crumbs
1 tablespoon Vermouth
1 tablespoon heavy cream
¼ teaspoon thyme

Preheat broiler. Remove and chop mushrooms stems, and sauté them in the butter along with the onion. Add the chicken, bread crumbs, seasoning, Vermouth and cream. Turn off the heat. Put the mushroom caps on a baking sheet, cut side down. Brush with butter. Broil for about two minutes. Invert and fill with stuffing. Brush with more melted butter and broil about three minutes longer. Serve immediately.

Layered California Sushi

4 cups rice
4 cups water
½ cup Japanese rice vinegar
½ cup sugar
1 teaspoon salt
½ cup mayonnaise mixed with wasabi paste (to taste)
1 to 2 ripe avocados, sliced or diced
Fresh lemon juice for rubbing the avocado
1 cucumber, peeled and cut lengthwise into thin strips, discarding the seeds
1 8-ounce package imitation crabmeat, shredded
4 7 x 9 inch sheets of toasted nori
wasabi paste as a condiment
Soy sauce as a condiment
Pickled ginger as a condiment

In a large heavy saucepan combine the rice with the water, bring the water to a boil, and simmer the rice, covered tightly, for 15 minutes or until water is absorbed and the rice is tender. Remove pan from heat, allow to sit, covered tightly, for 10 minutes, and transfer to a large bowl to cool. In a saucepan whisk together the vinegar, sugar and salt. Simmer the mixture until the sugar is dissolved.

Remove from heat and allow to cool. Sprinkle the seasoned vinegar over the rice to moisten it lightly, lifting and folding it carefully, so as not to mash the rice. Taste to see if there is enough flavor. Cover with a dampened cloth (do not chill). The rice can be made 3 hours in advance and kept at room temperature, covered with the dampened cloth.

Line a 9x13" pan with waxed paper. Layer two sheets of nori to cover bottom of pan. Spread half of the rice mixture evenly over nori sheets. Combine mayonnaise with wasabi paste, to taste. Spread over the rice. Top with the avocado, cucumber strips, and imitation crabmeat. Cover with remaining rice mixture. Top with two more sheets of nori, and press firmly with something flat, such as a large spatula. Flip onto a cutting board and slice through with a wet knife.

Note: The purpose of the wasabi paste is to mix with soy sauce. Start with small amounts of the wasabi, mixed with the soy sauce and taste. Keep adding the wasabi until it tastes more like the wasabi than the soy sauce. The ginger is used to cleanse the palate between bites. It does not take a lot of ginger to cleanse the palate.

Makes 12 to 18 servings

Pigs in a Blanket

1 8-ounce package refrigerated crescent rolls
3 tablespoons Durkee Famous Sauce
1 16-ounce package cocktail wieners

Preheat oven to 375 degrees. Unroll and separate crescent rolls. Roll out, one at a time, on a lightly floured surface. Roll to about ⅛-inch wide. Spread with "Durkee Famous Sauce." Cut each crescent roll into four slim strips. Wrap wieners in the strips, sealing the ends closed with cold water. Arrange seam-side down on ungreased baking sheet 2 inches apart. Bake 10-12 minutes until golden. Serve hot with or without a bowl of spicy sauce.
*Special Sauce recipe (page 84)

Stuffed Celery

1 8-ounce package cream cheese, softened
1 teaspoon Worcestershire Sauce
1 teaspoon celery seed
1 teaspoon Beau Monde seasoning
48 1-inch pieces of celery

Blend cream cheese, Worcestershire Sauce, celery seed, and Beau Monde seasoning until smooth. Fill hollows of each piece of celery. Serve chilled, or room temperature.

Finger Cheese Burgers

1½ pound ground beef
1 teaspoon seasoned salt
8 ounces sliced processed American cheese
½ stick of butter or margarine
8 hamburger buns, split
1 medium onion, sliced thin
12 cheery tomatoes, sliced thin

Preheat oven to 350 degrees. Mix ground beef and seasoned salt. Shape into twenty one-inch patties. Place in single layer in shallow baking pan. Bake in oven for about 5-6 minutes.

While burgers are baking, cut each cheese slice into quarters. Remove burgers from oven and place one piece of cheese on each patty. Return to oven and bake until cheese melts.

Blend butter and mustard in a saucepan over low heat. Toast buns in oven and spread with butter mixture. Cut each half into four triangles (like a pie).

Place each patty on a bun triangle; top with a slice of tomato and a slice of onion. Secure with toothpick. Serve immediately.

Makes 64 Appetizers

Ham Asparagus Roll-ups

2 10-ounce packages frozen asparagus, thawed
2 8-ounces packages cream cheese, softened
3 teaspoons horseradish
2 teaspoons Dijon mustard
½ teaspoon granulated garlic
1 teaspoon Worcestershire Sauce
1 pound ham, thinly sliced
Salt & pepper to taste

Cook asparagus until crisp-tender. Mix together cream cheese, horseradish, mustard, Worcestershire Sauce and garlic. Add salt and pepper to taste. On each slice of ham spread a thin layer of cheese mixture. Place one spear of asparagus at one end of ham slice and roll up, jelly roll-style. Chill for a couple of hours before serving.

Makes 24 Appetizers

Spicy Wieners & Bacon Roll-Ups

1 16-ounce package cocktail wieners
16 bacon slices, halved lengthwise

Special Sauce

¾ cup ketchup
¼ cup hot salsa
¼ cup brown sugar
⅛ teaspoon allspice

Preheat broiler. Combine sauce ingredients in a pan and cook over medium heat stirring until sugar is dissolved. Continue cooking for about 20 minutes, so the flavors are well blended. (The sauce can be made ahead and stored in refrigerator.)

Dip franks in sauce one by one, then wrap in bacon, securing with toothpicks. Broil franks about four inches from the heat, turning frequently. It may take 3-5 minutes before the bacon is well done.

Serve hot with toothpicks. Use the sauce for dipping.

Blue Cheese Liver Paté

8 ounces blue cheese
4 ounces cream cheese
1 4½-ounce can liver paté
⅛ teaspoon mace
4 tablespoons brandy
¼ teaspoon onion power

Blend all ingredients together well. Add the brandy and blend again. Chill and use as a spread with crackers.

Quick Liver Paté

1 pound chicken livers
2 large eggs, hard-boiled
1 tablespoon grated onion
¼ teaspoon mace
1 tablespoon brandy
⅛ teaspoon cayenne pepper
1 stick butter

Brown livers in ¼ stick of butter in a heavy fry pan, cook over medium heat until livers are pink inside (not well done). Put into food processor along with eggs, onion, mace, brandy, cayenne pepper and remaining butter. Pulse a few times. Do not over-process. Cover and chill overnight. Serve with crackers.

Liverwurst Paté Cheesecake

1 cup croutons, crushed
3 tablespoons butter, melted
1 package unflavored gelatin
½ cup white wine
2 8-ounce packages cream cheese, softened
1 8-ounce package good-quality liverwurst
¼ cup mayonnaise
¼ cup grated onion
1 tablespoon Dijon mustard
¼ cup fresh-squeezed lemon juice
3 tablespoons chopped pimiento-stuffed olives

Preheat oven to 350 degrees. In a medium bowl, combine crushed croutons and butter. Press onto the bottom of a 9-inch springform pan. Bake 8 to 10 minutes or until light brown. Remove from oven and let cool.

In a small sauce pan, soften gelatin in white wine. Over low heat, stir until gelatin is dissolved. Remove from heat and set aside. In a large bowl, combine cream cheese, liverwurst, and mayonnaise, mixing until well blended. Gradually add softened gelatin.

Stir in onion, mustard, lemon juice, and stuffed olives. Spread mixture over baked crust in the springform pan. Cover with plastic wrap and press gently to pack mixture. Refrigerate several hours or overnight until firm. To serve, uncover, remove pan sides, and place onto a serving plate. Serve with assorted crackers.

Country Paté with Prunes and Hazelnuts

2 bunches green onions, minced
2 cloves minced garlic
1 pound ground chicken or turkey
1 pound ground veal
1 pound ground pork
2 eggs beaten
5 ounces goat cheese, room temperature
1 cup fresh bread crumbs
3 tablespoons brandy
1 tablespoon kosher Salt
½ teaspoon ground allspice
½ teaspoon ground cardamom
½ teaspoon freshly-ground black pepper
¼ teaspoon dried thyme
About 18 dried and pitted prunes
½ cup hazelnuts, lightly toasted
Nonstick baking spray for pan

Preheat oven to 350 degrees. In a large mixing bowl, combine onions and garlic with the ground meats, eggs, goat cheese, bread crumbs, brandy, salt, allspice, cardamom, black pepper, and thyme.

Place ⅓ of this meat mixture in a paté mold or large loaf pan that has been sprayed with nonstick baking spray. Smooth the top of the mixture with spatula. Cover with the lightly toasted hazelnuts. Add another ⅓ of the meat mixture, again patting the surface smooth. Place the pitted prunes on top of this layer, about three to a row, six rolls total. Cover with the remaining meat mixture.

Place the paté-filled pan in a larger pan, and fill the larger pan with water until the liquid is about halfway up the side of the smaller pan. Bake for 1½ hours, or until the juices are almost clear. Remove from oven. Cool the paté for an hour, cover it with plastic wrap, then weight it with a brick or a large heavy can. Refrigerate overnight.

Remove the paté from the refrigerator and discard the plastic wrap. Run a sharp knife around the perimeter of the paté. Cover the pan with a serving platter and flip the pan and the platter upside down. The paté will slip out of the pan, ready for slicing. Serve with baguettes or your favorite crackers.

Crab Wonton Cups

2 green onions chopped (tops included)
4 ounces cream cheese, softened
⅓ cup Mayonnaise
4 ounces grated Parmesan cheese
2 teaspoons Old Bay Seasoning
1 teaspoon lemon juice
Paprika for garnish
⅔ cup crabmeat
12 wonton wrappers
1 tablespoon melted butter

Preheat the oven to 350 degrees. Prepare pan by spraying mini-muffin tins with cooking spray. To prepare filling, combine onions, cheeses and mayonnaise in a saucepan. Heat over low setting, stirring constantly until cheese has melted. Add lemon juice and gently fold in crabmeat. Remove from heat.

To prepare wontons, gently brush each wonton with butter before placing in mini-muffin tins. Let edges of wonton wrapper stick up from top of tins. Add filling to wonton wrappers and bake 12-15 minutes, till golden and crispy. Garnish filling with paprika.

Makes One Dozen Cups

Japanese Rumaki

¼ cup dry sherry
4 cloves minced garlic
1 tablespoon sesame oil
¼ cup soy sauce
¼ cup brown sugar
¼ teaspoon ground ginger
½ teaspoon curry power
1 pound chicken livers, rinsed & cut in half
1 8-ounce can whole water chestnuts
16 slices bacon, cut in half

Fold each piece of liver around a water chestnut. Wrap with a half-slice of bacon and fasten with toothpick. Mix the sauce ingredients together. Marinate the chicken liver bundles in this sauce for several hours, turning occasionally.

Place appetizers on shallow pan in preheated broiler. Turn frequently until bacon is thoroughly cooked, about 5-7 minutes. Serve hot.

Makes 32 Appetizers

Chinese Barbecued Chicken Wings

1½ dozen chicken wings
⅔ cup soy sauce
1 cup honey
½ teaspoon ginger
3 tablespoons red wine
2 clove minced garlic
½ teaspoon crushed red chili peppers

Preheat oven to 350 degrees. Remove wing tips from wings and then break each wing into two pieces. Place in a shallow pan. Cover and bake for 20-30 minutes. Remove pan from oven and pour off all grease. Mix sauce ingredients and pour over the wings. Bake uncovered for about 15-20 minutes, basting occasionally with sauce. Put chicken wings and all the sauce into a chafing dish. Serve.

Makes 36 Chicken Wings

Buffalo Wings

5 pounds chicken wings
4 cups peanut oil
½ stick of butter
1 cup Louisiana-brand hot sauce
1 tablespoon white wine vinegar

Chop off the tip of each wing and discard it, then chop wing in half, cutting at the joint to make two pieces. Heat oil to 375 degrees in a deep skillet or deep fryer, drop in half the wings and cook until they're golden and crisp. Remove to drain on paper towels. Cook remaining wings. Melt butter with hot sauce and vinegar in a saucepan over medium heat. Remove from heat. Place wings on a large serving platter. Pour the sauce over the wings to coat well. Serve with bowl of Bleu cheese dressing and celery sticks.

Makes 8-10 ½-pound servings

Oysters Rockefeller

36 fresh oysters in the half shell
6 tablespoons butter
1 bunch scallions, finely chopped
2 cups chopped fresh spinach
3 tablespoons finely chopped parsley
¼ cup cream
4 drops Tabasco sauce
1 teaspoon Pernod
Salt & pepper to taste
¼ cup freshly grated Parmesan cheese
⅓ cup bread crumbs
1 tablespoon chopped fresh tarragon
Rock salt
Lemon wedges for garnish

Preheat oven to 425 degrees. Using an oyster knife, pry open the oyster shells and remove the oysters. Drain the oysters, reserving the oyster liquor. Discard the top shells, scrub and dry the bottom shells. Melt butter in skillet over medium-high heat. Add scallions, spinach and parsley. Cook for about 3 to 4 minutes until spinach is wilted. Add cream, Tabasco, Pernod, and salt and pepper to taste. Cook over high heat for three to five minutes.

Remove from heat. Place a little of the reserved liquor on each oyster. Spoon the prepared spinach mixture evenly over each oyster shell, and spread to the rim.

Combine the Parmesan cheese, breadcrumbs, and tarragon in a small bowl. Sprinkle on top of the oysters. Pour rock salt onto a large baking sheet, about 1 inch deep. Arrange prepared oyster shells on top of the salt to steady them.

Bake in the preheated oven for about 10 minutes until the tops are golden and bubbly and the edges of the oysters begin to curl up. Serve immediately with lemon wedges and Tabasco Sauce.

Artichoke & Parmesan Swirls

1 package (17.3 ounces) puff pastry sheets, thawed
½ cup mayonnaise
½ cup grated Parmigiano-Reggiano cheese
1 teaspoon onion power
1 teaspoon garlic power
½ teaspoon ground black pepper
¼ cup finely chopped green onions
1 14-ounce can artichoke hearts, drained & chopped
1 egg, beaten

Preheat oven to 400 degrees. Stir the mayonnaise, cheese, onion power, garlic power, black pepper, onions and artichoke hearts together in a medium bowl. Unfold one pastry sheet on a lightly floured surface. Spread half the spinach mixture on the pastry to within one inch of the edge. Roll up like a jelly roll. Press the seam to seal. Repeat with the remaining pastry sheet.

Cut each roll into 20 half-inch slices, making 40 in all. Place on lightly greased baking sheets. Brush slices with beaten egg and bake for 15 minutes or until the pastries are golden brown. Remove the pastries from the oven and serve.

Makes 40 Appetizers

Olive Crisps

1 package (17.3 ounces) puff pastry sheets, thawed
1 egg, beaten
6 tablespoons tomato paste
6 tablespoons olive tapenade
½ cup Mozzarella cheese, shredded
½ cup Parmesan cheese, grated

Preheat oven to 400 degrees. Unfold one pastry sheet on a lightly floured surface and roll it into a 10 x 10-inch square. Spread half the tomato paste on the sheet. Top with half the tapenade. Sprinkle with half the mozzarella cheese and half the Parmesan cheese.

Starting at one side, roll up the sheet like a jelly roll, stopping half-way. Then roll up the opposite side to the center. Brush between the rolls with the egg and then press them together. Repeat with the remaining pastry sheet.

Cut each roll into twenty half-inch slices, making 40 in all. Place the slices, cut-side down, onto lightly greased baking sheets. Refrigerate for 20 minutes. Brush the slices with beaten egg, bake for 10 minutes or until the pastries are golden brown. Remove the pastries from baking sheet. Serve.

These are easily made in advance. Just put together and wrap in plastic and refrigerate until ready to bake.

Makes 40 Appetizers

Spinach Gruyere Puff Pastry

1 10-ounce package frozen chopped spinach, thawed
      & squeezed dry
6 tablespoons butter, divided
1 cup sliced fresh mushrooms
4 ounces Gruyere cheese, shredded
1 (17.3 ounces) package frozen puff pastry sheets,
      thawed
¼ teaspoon granulated garlic
¼ teaspoon thyme
¼ teaspoon salt
¼ teaspoon white pepper

Preheat oven to 400 degrees. Drain spinach well, pressing it between layers of paper towels to remove excess moisture. Melt 3 tablespoons butter in a skillet over medium heat, add the mushrooms and cook for 5 minutes. Mix together spinach, mushrooms, cheese, and spices and set aside. Roll one pastry sheet into a 13 x 11-inch rectangle. Melt remaining 3 tablespoons butter. Brush half the melted butter over pastry. Spread half of the spinach mixture over buttered pastry.

Roll up the pastry like a jelly roll, starting with the long side; repeat procedure with remaining pastry sheet, butter, and spinach mixture. Wrap rolls in plastic wrap and refrigerate up to two days if desired. Cut rolls into ¼-inch thick slices. Place on lightly greased baking sheets. Bake for 15 to 20 minutes, or until golden brown.

Makes 40 Appetizers

Spinach Diamond Puffs

1 10-ounce package frozen chopped spinach, thawed
      & squeezed dry
½ cup finely chopped carrots
¼ cup finely chopped green onions with tops
½ cup mayonnaise
¼ teaspoon ground nutmeg
¼ teaspoon salt
¼ teaspoon pepper
4 ounces Swiss cheese, shredded
1 17.3-ounce package puff pastry, thawed
1 egg, beaten

Preheat oven to 400 degrees. Combine spinach, carrots, onions, mayonnaise and seasonings in a bowl. Add shredded cheese and mix well. Lightly sprinkle a cutting board with flour. Roll half of pastry into a 12-inch square. Wrap remaining pastry in plastic wrap and refrigerate until ready to use. Cut pastry into sixteen 3-inch squares using a pizza cutter. Do not separate squares. Place a teaspoon of spinach mixture in center of each square. Flatten slightly with back of spoon. Brush beaten egg over cut lines in pastry and around outside edge of large square.

For each appetizer, bring two opposite corners of each square up over filling, pinch together firmly, and twist. Place on ungreased baking sheet and brush with beaten egg. Bake 17-18 minutes or until golden brown. Remove to serving platter. Repeat with remaining pastry sheet and spinach mixture. Serve warm.

Makes 32 Appetizers

Yard Long Party Sandwich

1 loaf French bread
12 ounces cream cheese, softened
¼ cup creamed horseradish
¼ cup grated onion
¼ teaspoon salt
1 teaspoon garlic power
1 pound sliced summer sausage, cut in strips
1 can of Spam, cut in thin strips
3 tomatoes, sliced very thin
1 8-ounce package pasteurized Swiss cheese slices
1 8-ounce package American cheese slices
Parmesan cheese (to sprinkle on top)
Pimento stuffed olives for garnish

Split bread lengthwise and hollow out each half. Be careful to leave a little bread dough right at bottom by crust. Mix cream cheese, horseradish, grated onion, salt and garlic power. Spread mixture on each hollowed out half.

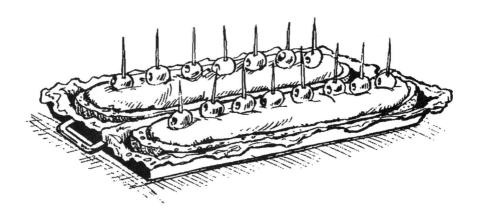

Sauté summer sausage and Spam in a non-stick skillet for 1-2 minutes. Arrange over the cream cheese mixture.

Place tomato slices on top of this, alternate one slice of American with one slice of Swiss cheese, laying them side by side and overlapping a little at the corners. Sprinkle with Parmesan cheese. Place on ungreased baking pan in a 400 degree preheated oven for about 10 minutes. Slice each half diagonally onto 8 pieces. Garnish with pimento-stiffed olives speared with toothpicks.

Makes 16 Appetizer Sandwiches

Marinated Ham & Swiss Finger Sandwiches

Marinade

1 cup (2 sticks) butter
¼ cup sweet onion, minced
½ teaspoon garlic power
1 tablespoon Worcestershire Sauce
2 tablespoon hot or spicy mustard
¼ cup brown sugar
1 tablespoon chopped fresh parsley

Sauté the onion in the butter over low heat in a small saucepan until the it's soft and translucent. Add the garlic power, Worcestershire Sauce, mustard and brown sugar. Stir until brown sugar is melted and well incorporated into the sauce. Remove from heat and stir in parsley. Set aside.

Sandwiches

24 2 x 2-inch small dinner rolls
Horseradish mayonnaise (I prefer Kraft Horseradish Sauce)
24 thin slices of deli ham or leftover bone-in ham
24 thin slices of Swiss cheese

Spray two 9 x 13-inch pans with a nonstick spray. Slice the rolls in half. Spread the top of the lower half of the split roll with a layer of Horseradish mayonnaise. Fold the ham slices to each roll. Next add a thin slice of Swiss cheese, also folded to fit the roll. Place these into two 9 x 13-inch baking pans. Top with the other half of the dinner roll. Pour marinate evenly over both pans of rolls. Cover tightly with foil and refrigerate overnight. Bake in a preheated 350 degree oven for twenty-five minutes. Remove foil and bake an additional ten minutes.

Makes 24 Appetizer Sandwiches

Baked, Brown Sugar Crusted, Bologna Finger Sandwiches

1 10-pound piece of good quality bologna
Salt & pepper to taste
1 cup brown sugar
4 dozen 2 x 2-inch dinner rolls
Whole grain mustard
Pickle slices

Preheat the oven to 200 degrees. Using a sharp knife, score the outside surface of bologna on the top and sides; lightly sprinkle with salt and pepper. Smear the brown sugar all over the bologna. Place the bologna on a rack in a roasting pan. Forget about bologna for at least 6-7 hours. You want the top and sides to be completely charred. Remove from oven and place on a large platter. Carve into thin slices and serve hot on rolls spread with whole grain mustard and garnished with a slice of pickle.

Makes 72 Appetizer Sandwiches

Herbed Vidalia Onion Tea Sandwiches

⅓ cup mayonnaise
½ cup minced fresh parsley leaves (¼ cup set aside)
2 tablespoons minced fresh tarragon leaves
Fresh lemon juice to taste
Tabasco to taste
12 thin slices of good quality white bread
1 Vidalia onion, sliced very thin

In a small bowl stir together the mayonnaise, ¼ cup of the parsley, the tarragon, the lemon juice, the Tabasco, and salt and pepper to taste. Spread one side of half of the bread slices with the mayonnaise mixture. Arrange the onion slices evenly over this. Top with the remaining bread slices. Press the sandwiches together gently. Remove crusts and cut into quarters. Put the remaining ¼ cup parsley on a plate and dip the edges of the sandwich quarters in the parsley for garnish.

Makes 24 Tea Sandwiches

Smoked Salmon & Caper Tea Sandwiches

1-8 ounce package cream cheese, softened
3 tablespoons red onion (finely dice)
2 tablespoons capers (drained)
8 slices Pumpernickel bread (or other black bread)
½ pound thinly sliced smoked salmon

Place cream cheese, red onion, and capers in a medium bowl, and stir with a rubber spatula until well mixed. Spread each slice of bread with cream cheese mixture. Arrange salmon in a thin layer over the cream cheese; top with a second slice of bread. Remove crusts, cut sandwiches in half and serve.

Makes 16 Tea Sandwiches

Deviled Egg Tea Sandwiches

1 8-ounce package cream cheese, softened
20 slices good quality bread
5 hardboiled eggs
1 8-ounce can sardines in oil
2 tablespoons mayonnaise
2 teaspoons mustard
1 tablespoon lemon juice
¼ teaspoon cayenne pepper (or to taste)

Spread 1 side of each slice of bread with cream cheese. Place remaining ingredients in a food processor. Pulse until a spread is formed. Spread the mixture evenly over 10 slices of bread. Top with the other 10 slices. Remove the crusts and cut into quarters.

Makes 40 Tea Sandwiches

Cucumber & Mint Tea Sandwiches

½ seedless cucumber, peeled and thinly sliced
    (about 32 slices)
¼ cup fresh mint leaves, finely chopped
¼ cup butter, softened
¼ cup cream cheese, softened
16 slices good quality cocktail-size bread

Place cucumber slices between layers of paper towels to remove excess moisture. In a small bowl, combine mint, butter, and cream cheese. Spread on one side of each slice of bread. Lay cucumber slices onto the buttered side of 8 slices of bread. Sprinkle with salt. Top with the remaining slices of bread. Cut each sandwich in half.

Makes 32 Tea Sandwiches

Cream Cheese & Pecan Tea Sandwiches

1 8-ounce package cream cheese, softened
¼ cup green pepper, finely chopped
⅓ cup onion, finely chopped
½ cup pecans, finely chopped
2 Tablespoons chili sauce
Salt & pepper to taste
1 16-ounce loaf thinly sliced, good quality white or wheat bread

Place into a bowl, and mix together well. Spread mixture on eight bread slices. Top with another slice of bread. Remove crusts, and cut into quarters. These you can make the day before and chill. Pile them on a platter and cover with saran wrap.

Makes 32 Tea Sandwiches

Curried Chicken Tea Sandwiches

2 cups cubed cooked chicken
1 medium unpeeled red apple, chopped
¾ cup dried cranberries
½ cup thinly sliced celery
¼ cup pecans, chopped
2 tablespoons green onion, thinly sliced
¾ cup mayonnaise
2 teaspoons lime juice
½ teaspoon curry power
12 slices good quality bread
lettuce leaves

In a bowl, combine the first six ingredients. Combine mayonnaise, lime juice and curry powder. Add to chicken mixture and stir to coat. Cover and refrigerate until ready to serve. Top with lettuce and chicken salad. Remove crusts and cut each slice of bread into quarters.

Makes 48 Tea Sandwiches

Chicken Salad & Smoked Almond Tea Sandwiches

3 cups chicken broth or water
2 whole boneless chicken breasts with skin
    (about 1½ pounds) halved
1 cup mayonnaise
⅓ cup minced shallot
1 teaspoon minced fresh tarragon leaves
24 very thin slices good quality white bread (or black
    bread)
½ cup smoked almonds (about 2 ounces) finely
    chopped

Place chicken breasts in one layer in a deep 12-inch skillet along with broth or water and bring to a boil. Reduce heat and poach chicken at a bare simmer for seven minutes, turning once. Remove skillet from heat and cool chicken in cooking liquid 20 minutes. Discard skin and finely shred then chicken.

In a bowl stir together chicken, ½ cup mayonnaise, shallots, tarragon, and salt and pepper to taste. Make 12 sandwiches with chicken salad and bread, pressing together gently. Remove the crust and cut each sandwich into quarters. Put almonds on a small plate and spread edges of sandwich quarters with remaining ½ cup mayonnaise to coat well. Roll edges in almonds. Sandwiches may be made 2 hours ahead, wrapped in plastic wrap, and chilled.

Makes 48 Tea Sandwiches

Savory Crab Cheesecake

25 crushed butter-flavored crackers (1 cup)
3 tablespoon melted butter
2 8-ounce packages cream cheese, softened
1 cup sour cream, divided
3 eggs beaten
¼ cup grated onion
1 teaspoon grated lemon peel
1 teaspoon seafood seasoning (Old Bay preferred)
¼ teaspoon cayenne pepper
⅛ teaspoon white pepper
1 cup crabmeat (flaked & cartilage removed)

Combine cracker crumbs and butter. Press into the bottom of 9-inch springform pan. Bake in a preheated 350 degree oven for 5 minutes. Remove from oven, and reduce heat to 325 degrees. In a food processor, blend cream cheese and ¼ cup sour cream until combined. Add onion, lemon peel, seafood seasoning, cayenne pepper and white pepper. Process until blended. Fold in the crabmeat. Pour over crust.

Place pan on baking sheet and bake for 35-40 minutes, or until center is almost a firm set. Turn off oven and leave cheesecake inside with door ajar for one hour. Remove from oven and allow too cool on a wire rack. Run knife around edge of pan to loosen. Spread remaining sour cream over top and refrigerate overnight. Unloosen sides of pan and allow cheesecake to stand at room temperature before slicing.

Makes 24 Appetizer Servings

Southwest Cheesecake

1½ cups finely crushed tortilla chips (hint of lime)
¼ cup melted butter
1 cup whole milk ricotta cheese
3 8-ounce packages cream cheese, softened
2½ cups (10 ounces) sharp cheddar cheese, shredded
1 can (4ounces) chopped green chilies, drained
3 cloves minced garlic
3 tablespoons tomato paste
1 teaspoon Mexican oregano
1½ teaspoon ground cumin
1 teaspoon granulated garlic
1 teaspoon chili powder
1 teaspoon ground coriander
¼ teaspoon cayenne pepper
¼ teaspoon salt
½ cup chopped cilantro
4 eggs
1 8-ounce carton sour cream
1 8-ounce jar jalapeño-cheddar cheese dip
1 cup chopped tomatoes, for garnish
½ cup chopped green onions, for garnish
¼ cup sliced black olives, for garnish
Sliced avocado, for garnish

Preheat oven to 325 degrees. Combine crushed tortilla chips and softened butter, and press into bottom of a lightly greased 9-inch springform pan. Bake at 325 degrees for 10 minutes. Cool on a wire rack. In the bowl of a food processor, combine ricotta cheese, cream cheese, chilies, garlic, tomato paste, spices and salt. Process until well blended. Add eggs, one at a time, mixing well before adding the next egg.

Fold in the cilantro. Pour into prepared pan. Place on a cookie sheet and bake for 60-70 minutes, until filling is just set. Combine sour cream and dip; mix thoroughly. Spread mixture over hot cheesecake; return to oven and continue baking for another 10 minutes. Turn off heat and allow cake to sit in oven with the door ajar for one hour. Remove from oven. Run a knife along the inside of pan to loosen. Unlatch to remove outer ring. Place on platter. Garnish with green onions, tomatoes, avocado and black olives. Cut into wedges and serve with salsa and chips.

(Note:This can be made days in advance and stored in refrigerator; it's delicious served at room temperature.)

Bacon, Gorgonzola Cheesecake with Parmesan Basil Crust

1 cup dried fresh bread crumbs
1 cup grated Parmesan cheese
¼ cup unsalted butter
1 teaspoon crushed dried basil
1 teaspoon salt
1 pound Gorgonzola cheese at room temperature
1 tablespoon minced garlic
3½ 8-ounce packages (28 ounces) cream cheese, softened
4 jumbo eggs at room temperature
½ cup heavy whipping cream
1 teaspoon hot pepper sauce
½ pound thick-cut bacon, diced & cooked crisp

Preheat oven to 325 degrees. Spray the bottom and sides of a 9-inch springform pan. Combine the bread crumbs, Parmesan cheese, dried basil, butter and salt in a medium bowl. Set aside ¼ cup for topping. Press remaining crumb mixture on to the bottom of the springform pan. Bake for 8-10 minutes.

Remove from oven and cool on wire rack. Combine Gorgonzola cheese, minced garlic, cream cheese, heavy cream and hot pepper sauce in the bowl of a food processor. Add the eggs, one at a time until well blended. Add the bacon and pulse to just mix. Do not over-process, as you want the bacon to add texture to the batter.

Pour on to the crust and sprinkle with reserved crumb mixture. Place pan on cookie sheet and bake for 60-75 minutes, until just set. Turn the oven off and leave the cheesecake inside the oven with the door ajar for one hour. Remove from oven and place on wire rack to cool completely. When cooled, release the sides of the pan.

Transfer to a serving platter. You can make this a couple of days in advance and store in the refrigerator. On the day you plan to serve this, have it sit at room temperature for at least 8 hours. Serve with fresh apple slices or toasted baguette slices.

Sweet & Savory Chevre Cheesecake with Biscotti Crust

Crust

6 ounces soft butter
1½ cups confectioner's sugar
2 cups all-purpose flour
1 cup biscotti crumbs

Filling

3 8-ounce packages cream cheese, softened
8 ounces mountain chevre goat cheese
4 eggs at room temperature
½ cup sugar
1 tablespoon chopped fresh rosemary
1 teaspoon salt
½ cup ground walnuts

Preheat oven to 325 degrees. Place butter, confectioner's sugar, flour, walnuts, and biscotti crumbs in a food processor. Pulse until finely ground. Do not over-process. Divide the crust between two 8-inch tart pans, being careful to press crust evenly on the bottom and sides of the pans. Place pans in refrigerator to chill for 30 minutes.

Next, place cream cheese and goat cheese in the food processor. Blend until smooth. Add eggs one at a time until well blended. Add sugar, rosemary and salt. Blend until incorporated. Remove chilled pans from the refrigerator and pour the batter into the pans. Place in oven and bake for 30-40 minutes. Check for doneness with a toothpick. The toothpick will come out clean when the cheesecake is set. If the batter is too soft, turn the oven off and allow cakes to remain in closed oven until firm. Remove from oven and place on wire rack to completely cool. Remove from pans and cut into wedges. Serve. (Can be made several days in advance and stored in refrigerator.)

Irresistible Gruyere Cheesecake

1 cup finely crushed rye crackers
3 tablespoons melted butter
12 ounces cream cheese, softened
1 16-ounce carton plain yogurt
2 jumbo eggs at room temperature
1 egg yolk
½ teaspoon crushed dried rosemary
½ teaspoon of dried caraway seed
2 cups (8 ounces) Gruyere cheese, shredded
½ teaspoon salt
½ teaspoon cayenne pepper
Assorted crackers

Preheat oven to 325 degrees. In a small bowl, combine cracker crumbs and butter. Press onto the bottom of a 9-inch springform pan that has been sprayed with a non-stick spray. Bake in oven for 8-10 minutes. Combine cream cheese, yogurt, egg yolk, rosemary, caraway seeds, salt and pepper in a food processor. Blend until smooth. Add eggs one at a time, blending well before adding the next egg. Add the Gruyere cheese, blend until just combined.

Pour onto crust and place on a cookie sheet. Bake for 60-70 minutes until center is almost set. Turn oven off and leave cheesecake inside for one hour with the door ajar. Remove from oven and place on wire rack to cool completely. Release sides of pan and serve immediately, or close up the sides and refrigerate overnight. When ready to serve, allow to sit at room temperature for several hours. Serve with crackers.

Beverages

Refreshing Champagne Punch

1 12-oz can frozen punch, partially thawed
1 10-oz package frozen strawberries
⅔ cup orange juice
2 Tablespoons lemon juice
24 ounces ginger ale
1 bottle of champagne
3 cups club soda

Place a frozen ice ring in a punch bowl. Pour in the fruit punch, water, strawberries and juice. Stir to dissolve the pinch. Slowly add the ginger ale and champagne.

Makes 25 4-ounce servings

Tropical Rum Punch

2 quarts of guava nectar
6 cups unsweetened pineapple juice
1 cup fresh lime juice
2 cups coconut cream
1 750-ml bottle of Light Malibu Rum (or to taste)

Chill all ingredients well in a large punch bowl. Float an ice mold or block of ice. Serve over crushed ice, if desired.

Makes 40 4-oz servings

Ginger Rum Punch

½ cup brown sugar, packed
½ cup water
1 large thumb-size piece fresh ginger, chopped
5 cups unsweetened pineapple juice
1½ cups amber rum
2 liters (about 8½ cups) grapefruit soda
4-6 cups club soda

Chill all ingredients well before mixing. In a medium saucepan, bring the brown sugar, water, and ginger to boil. Lower the heat and simmer for 15 or 20 minutes. Cool. Strain the ginger from the brown sugar mixture and pour the sugar-water into the punch bowl. Stir in the pineapple juice and add the rum. Just before serving, stir in the grapefruit soda and club soda. Float an ice mold. Serve over crushed ice, if desired.

Makes 40 4-oz Servings

Tequila Punch

1 quart Tequila (4 cups)
4 750-ml bottles of Sauterne (13 cups)
1 750 ml bottle of champagne (3 ¼ cups)
Simple syrup*
8 cups fresh melon balls or cubes and/or a Lime Ice
    Mold

Chill all ingredients well before mixing. Pour all ingredients but the fruit into a large punch bowl and sweeten to taste with simple syrup. Add fruit, if desired, or float an ice mold.

*Simple syrup: Heat equal parts sugar and water to boiling in a small sauce pan. Reduce heat and continue cooking for just a minute of two. Cool.

Makes 40 4-oz servings

Sangria Punch

3 fresh peaches, peeled and seeded
1 cup strawberries or other fruit of your choice
    (optional)
1 cup simple syrup, (see below) or to taste
2 cups orange juice
½ cup lime juice
½ cup brandy or peach brandy
½ cup Cointreau
3 750-ml bottles of dry red wine (10 cups)
1 orange, thinly sliced
2 limes, thinly sliced
1 quart club soda (4 cups) or 1 bottle champagne

Puree the peaches and strawberries in a blender or food processor. Combine the pureed fruit and simple syrup. Stir in the orange juice, brandy, Cointreau, and wine. Add the sliced citrus fruit pieces. Stir and chill well in the refrigerator. Just

Bombay Punch

2 cups fresh-squeezed lemon juice
Powdered sugar or simple syrup to taste
3 cups brandy
3 cups dry sherry
⅓ cup maraschino juice
⅓ cup orange liqueur
3 750-ml bottles champagne
1 quart club soda
Ice mold

Chill all ingredients well before mixing. Sweeten the lemon juice to taste with sugar or simple syrup. Transfer to a punch bowl. Stir in the brandy, sherry, maraschino, and orange liqueur. Add the champagne and club soda last. Stir. Float an ice mold. If desired, garnish with slices of orange or lemon.

Makes 40 4-oz servings

Open House Punch

1 750-ml bottle Southern Comfort
1 6-ounce can lemon juice
1 6-ounce can frozen lemonade
1 6-ounce can of frozen orange juice
3 liters 7-Up or Sprite

Chill ingredients. Mix first four ingredients in a large punch bowl. Add 7-Up or Sprite. Add drops of red food coloring as desired, and stir. Float block of ice, garnish with fruit slices.

Makes 32 4-oz servings

Chi-Chi Punch

1 gallon vodka
1 gallon pineapple juice
1¼ quarts pineapple juice
3½ quarts Coco Lopez
2 quarts lemon juice
84 fresh pineapple chunks

Combine all ingredients chill.

Makes 84 4-oz servings

Champagne Slush

1 pint of Rum

2 750-ml bottles of champagne

3 6-ounce cans of frozen lemonade concentrate, thawed

6 12-ounce cans of ginger ale

Combine ingredients in a large container and mix well. Freeze until firm. Thaw slightly before serving.

Makes 18 4-oz servings

Vodka Lime Punch

2 12-ounce cans of frozen limeade

6 limes, sliced

1 liter vodka

2 liters 7-Up

In large punch bowl, place limeade and 7-Up. Stir well. Add vodka and lime slices. Place block of ice into punch bowl and allow too chill for 15 minutes.

Makes 36 4-oz servings

Piña Colada Punch

Ice Ring

> 1 8-ounce can pineapple chunks, drained
> Maraschino cherries

Prepare ice ring in advance. Fill ring mold with water to within one inch of rim; freeze. Arrange pineapple chunks and maraschino cherries on top of ice. Carefully pour small amount of cold water over fruit; freeze.

Punch

> 1 20-ounce can crushed pineapple
> 1 15-ounce can cream of coconut
> 1 46-ounce can pineapple juice, chilled
> 1 pint dark rum (or to taste)
> 1 32-ounce bottle club soda, chilled

In blender container, combine crushed pineapple and cream of coconut; blend until smooth. Put this mixture into a large punch bowl and add the pineapple juice and rum. Just before serving, add club soda and ice ring.

Makes 24 to 30 4-oz servings

Festive Milk Punch

¾ cup sugar
1 liter whiskey
7 quarts milk
½ teaspoon nutmeg

Mix all ingredients in a large kettle. Pour over large block of ice in large punch bowl.

Makes 64 4-oz servings

Whiskey Sour Punch

4 liters lemon sour
12 lemons, sliced
½ cup Grenadine syrup
2 liters whiskey

Place block of ice into large punch bowl. Over this, pour whiskey, syrup and lemon sour. Stir. Garnish with lemons.

Makes 50 4-oz servings

Cranberry Punch

1 46-ounce bottle cranberry juice cocktail, chilled
1 6-ounce can frozen orange juice
1 liter gin
1 liter 7-Up
1 orange, sliced

In large punch bowl, place juices and gin. Stir well. Place a large block of ice into punch bowl. Add 7-Up just before serving. Garnish with orange slices.

Makes 24 4-oz servings

Eye Opener Punch

2 quarts orange juice
1 liter Rhine wine
2 liters light rum
2 cups sugar
½ cup lemon juice
2-3 oranges, sliced

Mix juices, wine and rum. Taste before adding sugar. Place a large block of ice in large punch bowl. Add mixture and stir well. Garnish with orange slices.

Makes 42 4-oz servings

Daiquiri Punch

1½ quarts cracked ice
1 12-ounce can limeade concentrate
1 750 ml bottle light rum

Place ice in large punch bowl. Add limeade and rum. Stir well. Strain into cocktail glasses and serve at once.

Makes 24 4-oz servings

Luau Punch

2 46-ounce cans unsweetened pineapple juice
2 quarts orange juice
½ can crème de coconut
2 cups lemon juice
2 cups sugar
2 liters dark rum
1 orange, sliced
1 lemon, sliced
2 medium bananas, sliced thin
2 liters ginger ale

In large punch bowl, place fruit juices, sugar, fruit slices, and crème de coconut. Stir well until sugar is dissolved. Add rum. Allow mixture to ripen at room temperature for 1 hour. Place a large block of ice into bowl. Add ginger ale just before serving.

Makes 32 4-oz servings

Saturday Night Punch

1 quart orange juice
2 cups lemon juice
2 cups lime juice
2 cups sugar
½ cup grenadine
2 lemons, thinly sliced
2 limes, thinly sliced
2 750-ml bottles of whiskey
1 liter club soda

Place fruit juices and sugar into a large punch bowl. Stir until sugar dissolves. Add the whiskey and the fruit slices. Allow to ripen in refrigerator for 1 hour. Place a large block of ice into punch bowl. Right before serving, pour in the club soda.

Makes 30 4-oz servings

Banana Euphoria Bowl

10 medium-size ripe bananas
1 cup sugar
1 cup lime juice
1 750-ml bottle light rum
10 ounces 151 proof rum
1 quart plus 12 ounces pineapple juice
12 ounces mango nectar
3 limes, sliced

Cut 8 bananas into thin slices and place in electric blender with lime juice and sugar. Blend well until smooth. Add both kinds of rum, pineapple juice, and nectar. Stir well. Cut remaining bananas into thin slices. Cut lime into thin slices. Float both banana and lime slices on punch. Allow ingredients to ripen at room temperature for about 1 hour. Place large block of ice into punch bowl and serve.

Makes 24 4-oz servings

Raspberry Delight

1quart pineapple juice
1 liter ginger ale
1 quart pineapple sherbet
1 quart raspberry sherbet
1 liter rum

Blend ingredients together in a large punch bowl, stir until well blended. Add rum to taste. Serve over crushed ice.

Makes 24 4-oz servings

Eggnog

4 egg yolks
⅔ cup sugar
2 quarts milk, scalded and then allowed to cool
1 teaspoon vanilla extract
1 teaspoon cinnamon
4 egg whites
4 tablespoons sugar
2 cups bourbon

Beat sugar into egg yolks. Slowly stir in milk. Cook in double boiler over hot (not boiling) water, stirring constantly until mixture coats spoon. Cool, add vanilla, spices and whiskey. Beat egg whites until foamy. Gradually add 4 tablespoons sugar, beating until soft peaks form. Fold into punch bowl; chill 3-4 hours.

Makes 12 4-oz servings

Party Vodka Punch

1 ice ring or block of ice
1 12-ounce can orange juice concentrate
1 12-ounce can lemonade concentrate
2 cups sugar
1 750-ml bottle of vodka
1 quart club soda
1 quart ginger ale
Sliced oranges, lemons & limes

Reconstitute orange juice and lemonade. Mix 2 cups sugar and 2 cups water in a medium saucepan. Heat until sugar is thoroughly dissolved. When cooled, add to fruit juices. (The dissolved sugar is the secret of the punch.) Add the vodka. Just before serving, add: 1 quart club soda, 1 quart ginger ale, and sliced fruit to the punch bowl. Garnish with maraschino cherries or strawberries for each serving.

Makes 24 4-oz servings

Triple Fruit Jamboree

1 quart unsweetened pineapple juice
1 quart orange juice
2 cups lemon juice
1 quart unsweetened grapefruit juice
2 cups sugar
1 750-ml bottle of gin
1 lemon, sliced
1 orange, sliced
2 cups drained pineapple chunks
1 liter club soda

In a large punch bowl, place the fruit, fruit juices and sugar. Stir until sugar is dissolved. Add the gin. Allow ingredients to ripen at room temperature for about 1 hour. Place a large block of ice into punch bowl. Add the club soda just before serving.

Makes 42 4-oz servings

Friday Night Punch

4 cups sugar
4 cups water
2 quarts lemon juice
1 1.75 liter bottle dark rum
Lemon slices

Place sugar and water in large saucepan. Heat and stir until sugar dissolves. Pour into large punch bowl, adding remaining ingredients. Allow to ripen for 2 hours at room temperature. Add a large block of ice and mix gently. Garnish with lemon slices.

Makes 24 4-oz servings

Fish House Punch

4 cups sugar
4 cups water
2 quarts lemon juice
1 liter dark rum
½ liter brandy
Lemon slices

Place sugar and water in large saucepan. Heat and stir until sugar dissolves. Pour into large punch bowl, adding remaining ingredients. Allow to ripen for 2 hours at room temperature. Add a large block of ice and mix gently. Garnish with lemon slices.

Makes 36 4-oz servings

Morning After Punch

1 12-ounce can frozen grapefruit juice concentrate
1 12-ounce can frozen orange juice concentrate
1 liter gin
2 oranges, sliced
12 Maraschino cherries
½ teaspoon ginger
2 liters ginger ale

In a large punch bowl, place fruit juices and liquor. Stir.
Add the fruit and ginger. Allow to ripen in refrigerator. Place
a block of ice in the bowl. Add the ginger ale just before
serving.

Makes 24 4-oz servings

Everybody Welcome Punch

2 liters whiskey
1 12-ounce can frozen lemonade concentrate
1 12-ounce can frozen orange juice concentrate
1 12-ounce can frozen limeade concentrate
2 liters lemon lime soda

In large punch bowl, place whiskey and fruit juices. Stir well.
Allow to ripe in refrigerator. Place a large block of ice in
punch bowl. Add the soda just before serving.

Makes 24 4-oz servings

Blackberry Brandy Punch

1 liter blackberry brandy
1 liter ginger ale
16 ounces lemon-lime soda
2½ cups unsweetened pineapple juice
1 orange, sliced
1 lemon, sliced

In a large punch bowl, combine all ingredients except ginger ale and lemon lime soda. Allow to ripen in refrigerator. Place a large block of ice into punch bowl and stir. Add soda pop just before serving.

Makes 25 4-oz servings

Mint Julep Punch

1 cup mint jelly
4 cups water
1 750-ml bottle of bourbon
6 cups pineapple juice
½ cup lime juice
7 cups lemon-lime soda

Chill all ingredients well before mixing. Combine mint jelly and 2 cups of water in a saucepan, stirring over low heat until jelly melts, cool. Add bourbon, pineapple juice, remaining water and lime juice, chill. Pour mixture over a block of ice in a punch bowl. Slowly pour in soda. Garnish with lime slices and mint leaves.

Makes 44 4-oz servings

Tea Punch

2 quarts boiling water
8 tea bags
¼ teaspoon allspice
¼ teaspoon nutmeg
¼ teaspoon cinnamon
2 cups super-fine sugar
4 oranges, sliced
9 lemons, sliced
2 liters ginger ale

In a large heavy kettle, place all ingredients except ginger ale. Stir until sugar is dissolved. Cool 1-2 hours. Pour equal amounts of the tea and ginger ale over a block of ice in large punch bowl.

Makes 24 4-oz servings

Orange Sherbet Punch

½ gallon orange sherbet
2 quarts orange juice
2 liters orange soda pop

Put sherbet into large punch bowl. Add equal amounts of orange juice and soda pop. Garnish with orange slices.

Makes 15 4-oz servings

Raspberry Fizzle

½ gallon raspberry sherbet
1 quart cranberry juice
1 quart orange juice
1 liter ginger ale
1 pint fresh or 1 10-ounce bag frozen raspberries

Put sherbet into a large punch bowl. Add the juices and raspberries. Add the ginger ale. Ladle into punch cups.

Makes 10 4-oz servings

Quick & Easy Punch

½ gallon lime sherbet
1 Can Hi C "Citrus" Drink
2 liters 7-Up

Put sherbet into a large punch bowl. Add equal amounts of the liquid, pouring slowly down the side of the bowl. Ladle into punch cups.

Makes 15 4-oz servings

Orange Dream Sickle Punch

1 quart vanilla ice cream
2 pints orange sherbet
1-16 ounce can lemon lime flavored soda
1 quart cold milk

Place the ice cream and sherbet in a punch bowl. Pour in the milk and lemon-lime soda. Stir gently and serve immediately.

Makes 24 4-oz servings

Eggnog Wassail

3 quarts eggnog
1½ quarts apple cider
½ teaspoon ground nutmeg
½ teaspoon ground cinnamon
4 whole cloves

Combine eggnog, cider and spices in large pot. Heat on low stirring occasionally. Remove cloves and pour into glasses. Serve hot or cold.

Makes 8 4-oz servings

White Cranberry Peach Party Punch

1 64-ounce bottle white cranberry juice and peach
   juice drink (chilled)
8 ounces lemon-lime soda
4 ounces orange juice
1 pint lime or orange sherbet, softened

Combine all ingredients, except sherbet, in large punch bowl. Gently stir. Float softened sherbet on top of punch just before serving.

Makes 15 4-oz servings

Festive Party Punch

3 3-ounce packages fruit-flavored gelatin mix
4 cups white sugar
13 cups boiling water
2 46-ounce cans pineapple juice
1 16-ounce bottle lemon juice
2 liters ginger ale

In a large bowl, combine gelatin and sugar. Stir in boiling water until mixture is dissolved. Stir in pineapple juice and lemon juice concentrate. Divide into two containers and freeze until solid. To serve, place gelatin mixture in punch bowl and chop into pieces. Pour in ginger ale.

Makes 40 4-oz servings

Pineapple Delight

1 12-ounce can frozen orange juice concentrate
3 cups water
1 46-ounce can pineapple juice
1 liter ginger ale

In a large punch bowl, combine orange juice, water and pineapple juice; chill. Stir in ginger ale just before serving.

Makes 24 4-oz servings

Cherry Fruit Punch

3 quarts orange juice
3 cups lemon juice
1 cup Maraschino cherries with juice
4 quarts sparkling white grape juice
2 oranges, sliced

Mix orange and lemon juice with the cherries. Put a large block of ice into large punch bowl. Add fruit mixture, then pour in grape juice. Garnish with the orange slices.

Makes 24 4-oz servings

Triple Fruit Jubilee

⅔ cup sugar
3 cups grapefruit juice
3 cups orange juice
1 gallon peach nectar
1 tablespoon grated orange peel
2 pinches nutmeg
2 liters club soda

Mix sugar and grapefruit in a large kettle until sugar is dissolved. Mix in remaining ingredients excluding soda. Place in large punch bowl over large block of ice. Add soda right before serving. Garnish with orange slices.

Makes 24 4-oz servings

Trapper's Punch

2 cups orange juice
2 cups lemon juice
2 cups Grenadine syrup
2½ liters ginger ale

Put a large block of ice in punch bowl. Pour juices and Grenadine syrup over ice to chill. Just before serving add the ginger ale. If desired, garnish with fresh berries.

Makes 12 4-oz servings

Apple Punch

3 quarts apple juice
4 cinnamon sticks
1 teaspoon ground cloves
3 cups pineapple juice
1 cup lemon juice
1 quart orange juice
2 liters ginger ale

Place apple juice and spices in heavy saucepan. Simmer uncovered for 15 minutes, then mix the spiced juice with remaining fruit juices. Chill in refrigerator. When ready to serve, place a large block of ice into punch bowl. Pour in the ginger ale.

Makes 24 4-oz servings

Hot Mulled Cider

1 cup brown sugar
¼ teaspoon salt
1 teaspoon ground cloves
4 cinnamon sticks
2 dashes nutmeg
½ gallon apple cider

Combine ingredients in a heavy saucepan. Slowly bring to a boil and simmer about 20 minutes. Remove cinnamon sticks. Serve hot, garnished with orange slices.

Makes 10 4-oz servings

Hot Vanilla Cocktail

1 teaspoon vanilla
1½ ounces whiskey
1 cup milk
½ teaspoon cinnamon
⅛ teaspoon nutmeg
Sugar to taste

Combine all ingredients in saucepan. Heat through till hot.

Makes 1 serving

Hot Kahlula Cocktail

1 ounce Kahlula
1 ounce whiskey
8 ounces milk
½ teaspoon cinnamon
¼ teaspoon cinnamon
¼ teaspoon nutmeg

In saucepan, place milk and spices. Heat through until milk is scalded but not boiled. Add Kahlula and whiskey. Serve hot.

Makes 1 serving

Hot Crème de Menthe Cocktail

1 ounce crème de menthe
1 ounce gin
1 cup milk
⅛ teaspoon nutmeg
⅛ teaspoon cinnamon

Combine all ingredients in sauce pan. Heat through, but do not boil. Remove from heat when hot. Pour into hefty mug, serve hot.

Makes 1 serving

Hot Free & Easy Punch

20 cinnamon sticks
2 quarts grape juice
1 quart boiling water
½ cup lemon juice
⅛ teaspoon ground nutmeg
1 liter gin

Tie the cinnamon and nutmeg in cheesecloth and place the bag in a large kettle (not aluminum) with the other ingredients (except the gin). Simmer, uncovered, stirring occasionally, 10-15 minutes. Then add gin to taste (up to 1 liter.) Discard spice bag. Serve hot.

Makes 24 4-oz servings

Hot Buttered Rum

1½ ounces dark rum
6 ounces apple cider
1 tablespoon butter
1 tablespoon brown sugar
1 cinnamon stick
pinch of nutmeg

Combine first four ingredients in a saucepan. Heat at low temperature until butter and sugar are dissolved. Pour into mug and garnish with cinnamon stick and nutmeg. Serve hot! (Option: Garnish with hot cinnamon candy.)

Makes 1 serving

Hot Spiked Orange Tea

1 cup powdered orange-flavored beverage mix
¼ cup instant tea power
1 3-ounce package sweetened lemonade mix
1 cup sugar
1 teaspoon cinnamon
Whiskey (added later to taste)

Mix all ingredients except whisky and store in airtight container. To make 1 cup, place 1 tablespoon of mixture in a cup. Pour in boiling water and stir until dissolved. Add whiskey to taste; serve hot.

Makes 1 serving

Hot Irish Coffee

1 cup strong coffee
Dash cinnamon
Pinch of dried mint leaves
1½ ounces whiskey
1 ounce whipped cream

Make sure coffee is hot! Add cinnamon and mint. Mix well until flavors ripen. Add whiskey. Light with match, allow too burn out. Garnish with whipped cream.

Makes 1 serving

Notes

Notes

Notes

Notes

Notes